D1349388

PICTURE HISTORY OF WORLD ART

PICTURE HISTORY OF WORLD ART

Hamlyn
London · New York · Sydney · Toronto

Nathaniel Harris

Published by
The Hamlyn Publishing Group Limited
London · New York · Sydney · Toronto
Hamlyn House, Feltham, Middlesex, England
© Copyright The Hamlyn Publishing Group Limited 1973
First published 1973
Second impression 1974

ISBN 0 600 36998 6

Phototypeset in England by
Filmtype Services Limited, Scarborough
Printed in Italy by
Officine Grafiche Arnoldo Mondadori, Verona

Endpapers Van Gogh: Starry Night (detail). Pen and ink drawing.
Kunsthalle, Bremen.

Half-title page Picasso: Study for the ballet 'Mercury'. Graphite drawing.

Title page Chinese Ming dynasty landscape (detail), probably by Chou
Ch'en. Ink and colour on paper. Freer Gallery of Art, Washington.

Below 13th-century builders at work. Drawing in the 'Book of St Alban'.
Trinity College, Dublin.

Opposite Michelangelo: Prisoner. Sketch. Accademia, Florence.

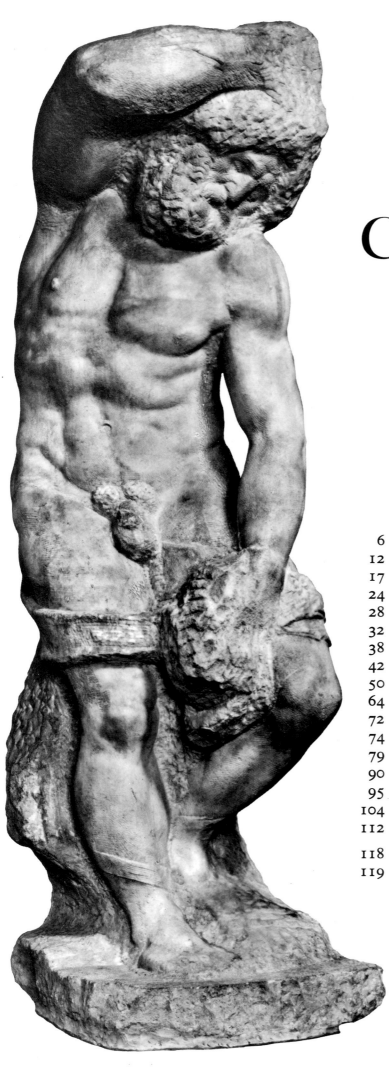

Contents

The First Artists

One of the remarkable things about human beings is their urge to make images and patterns. Men were painting, scratching out designs and carving figures long before they discovered how to grow crops, write, or build and organise towns. So although art serves no 'practical' purpose, it can hardly be classed as a luxury: it must satisfy a real and pressing inner need. Nobody has succeeded in defining precisely what that need is, any more than they have succeeded in explaining why certain arrangements of shapes and colours satisfy it; but it undoubtedly forms part of man's drive to explore, interpret and finally reshape his own being and the world about him. The history of art is simply a record of some of his efforts to do so.

The first works of art must have been produced as a result of some important advance in mental or spiritual awareness. This happened long ago in ordinary terms, but only quite recently in human history. Men have lived on earth for a million years, most of it spent developing tools and weapons, and making themselves efficient hunters – an unimpressively slow process which was none the less the first step towards mastery over nature. Objects that are unmistakably works of art date back little more than thirty thousand years. The earliest artists we know of were Stone Age hunters who entered Europe from Asia during the last great Ice Age, in pursuit of mammoth and other big game; perhaps it was the shock of the intense cold, and dread of the vast continental forest, that prompted them to scratch pictures on bone and carve stone and ivory statuettes of women and animals. Some of these must have been made as an effort to control the mysterious powers that ruled an unfriendly universe. Many of the female figures are certainly magical objects, intended to ensure the fertility of the individual or group. Their sexual and maternal characteristics are emphasised, and all other features – arms, legs, faces – are only suggested or left out altogether. The 'Venus of Savignano' [2], for example, is all breasts, belly, thighs and buttocks – not a person but an animal dedicated to breeding.

Rock surfaces gave prehistoric man a large natural canvas on which he could paint, draw and carve. The best-preserved examples of early painting have been found deep in caves at Lascaux, Altamira and other sites in south-west France and northern Spain. The art created here, which reached its climax about 12,000

1 Animals of the chase. About 15,000–10,000 BC. Lascaux, France.
2 The Venus of Savignano. About 25,000 BC. Museo Preistorico Pigorini, Rome.

BC, is a magical hunter's art. The cave painter rarely concerned himself with anything but the animals his group hoped to track down and kill. He 'captured' them by catching their likeness, probably strengthening his power over them by means of spells and ceremonies; the element of magical wish-fulfilment is often emphasised by the flying arrows and traps he included in the picture. The best cave paintings are so vivid and accurate that they must be the result of long practice and the handing on of skills from generation to generation – an impression confirmed by the fact that they range from crude and static outline drawings to vigorous, lively studies in which the beast is modelled in several carefully shaded colours. This is often evident on a single surface, as in the illustration from Lascaux [1]; the prehistoric artist seems to have worked on any available free space, if necessary overlapping the paintings of his predecessors and ignoring differences

3 Rock painting in the 'Second Hunter style' at Casas Viejas, near Cadiz.

4 Painted jar from Ning-ting-hsien, Kansu, China. 2nd millennium BC. Museum für Völkerkunde, Munich

5 Stonehenge. Finished about 1500 BC.

in scale between the old and the new. Several men must have worked on these paintings of a horse, cattle and deer, which were done in red ochre and charcoal at different times and in distinct styles.

The Lascaux paintings represent one of the most important approaches to art: an attempt to reproduce faithfully what the artist can see. This approach is called realism or naturalism. Another, equally valid approach is expressionism–communication of the artist's feelings or attitudes by distorting or emphasising particular aspects of the visible world. The Venus of Savignano is one example; another is the rock art of eastern Spain, produced some 6,000 years later than Lascaux. In this expressionistic 'Second Hunter style' [3], men and animals are reduced to cartoon-like silhouetted figures grouped in dynamic battle and hunting scenes; all the emphasis is on excitement, action and movement.

This style of painting probably started in one of the earliest of all cities, Çatal Hüyük, in what is now Turkey. Cities grew up after one of the most important events in human history: the discovery of agriculture. Starting in south-west Asia from about 9000 BC, men began to cultivate cereals and to domesticate animals. Farming began to replace hunting, providing a settled existence, a regular food supply, and more leisure; and this in turn called into being market towns linked by a network of international trade. The city is the nucleus of civilisation, favourable alike to art and invention. Here men began to harden clay vessels with fire, and later to bake them in kilns. The new art of pottery, of tremendous practical value, spread rapidly along the routes of trade and migration, and was soon widely practised.

Again men were not content with producing useful objects: long before the invention of the potter's wheel, vessels were elegantly shaped, polished, and painted. This white pot with black and red painted decorations [4] is an example of a third approach to art, on a par with naturalism and expressionism: pure abstraction, in which the artist combines shapes, patterns and colours to create satisfying designs with no counterpart in everyday reality.

All the arts were soon pressed into the service of religion. In the third millennium (3000–2000) BC, the people of the Mediterranean area and the Balkans made

4

5

clay statuettes of the 'Great Mother'. Later, artists in the Cycladic islands of the Aegean carved figurines in which geometrical shapes and lines replaced realism, and these were imitated by the Sardinians and other Mediterranean peoples. An elaborate cult of the dead, which led its devotees to build tombs and other monuments constructed with stone slabs, spread along the Mediterranean and into north-west Europe. The finest of these megalithic ('big stone') structures is to be found in Britain, on Salisbury Plain: Stonehenge [5], at once a temple complex and astronomical observatory, is a remarkably sophisticated group that still provokes heated arguments among experts as to where the stones came from, how they were transported, and exactly what their arrangement means.

With the rise of civilisations in the Near East and China, less advanced peoples over huge areas fell more or less under their influence and became cultural, if not political, tributaries; the megalithic style itself owes a good deal to the death-obsessed art of Egypt (see page 15). Later chapters of this book are therefore inevitably concerned with the arts of the great civilisations. But here it is worth noticing the role of the nomadic tribes whose descendants still roam the vast steppe area from China to eastern Europe. Though widely different in origin, they share a common, highly mobile way of life which led them to create portable

works of art, and in particular decorated weapons, riding equipment and personal ornaments of bronze and gold [6]. The chief features of their decorations are animals, sometimes realistically observed, sometimes distorted into almost unrecognisable designs. These peoples acted as unconscious carriers between distant settled communities, taking over ideas and images from one and passing them on to others. In this way the 'Barbarians', so often blamed for the destruction of nations and civilisations, made a great contribution to the development of civilisation itself.

The arts of prehistoric man have been practised down to modern times among the ever-diminishing population of 'primitive' peoples. In this century African Bushmen and Australian Aborigines have made rock paintings. Pacific and African Negro art descend directly from the Stone Age farmers; the ubiquitous masks and sculpted wooden figures are part of the apparatus of ancestor worship, just like the megalithic tombs of Europe. This is not to say that they are therefore obsolete or incomprehensible: art does not 'progress'—or at least not in same sense as, say, technology. 'Primitive' works like the Congolese female mask [7], with its simplified lines and bare surfaces, have deeply influenced modern artists. They suggest that good art possesses fundamental qualities that outlast changes in technique and fashion.

6

6 Gold belt plaque from Siberia, made by a Nomad craftsman.
4th–3rd centuries BC. Hermitage, Leningrad.

7 Bapende female mask from Kwango, Congo. 19th century AD.
Museum für Völkerkunde, Munich.

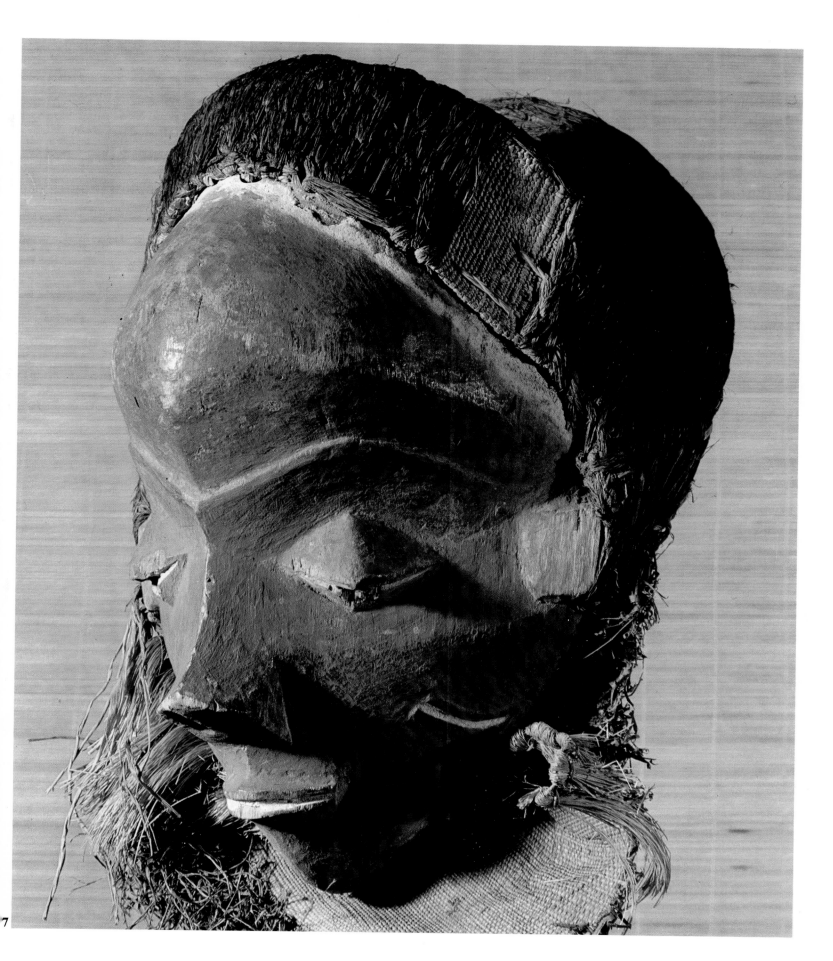

7

The Ancient World

The first civilisations arose among farming communities settled along great rivers in Asia and Africa: the Tigris and Euphrates in Mesopotamia (modern Iraq), the Nile in Egypt, and the Yellow River in China.

Civilisation creates a demand for more art—for buildings and decorations, and for objects, carvings and pictures in the service of gods, kings and nobles. With this, craftsmen and artists emerged as a separate professional class, and soon developed highly specialised skills and traditional techniques.

The skill they developed is well illustrated by a gold wig helmet [8] from Ur in Mesopotamia, made four and a half thousand years ago; the stylised engraved hair, the bun and the carefully modelled ears are the work of a confident well-trained professional.

Ur was one of the cities of Sumer, the first civilisation in human history, which appeared in Mesopotamia around 3500 BC. Much Sumerian art was religious, and quantities of small statues intended as temple offerings have survived.

Sumerians, Akkadians, Babylonians, Kassites, Assyrians and Persians came down upon the fertile land of Mesopotamia, conquered, settled down, and were in turn conquered by vigorous new peoples. The most warlike were undoubtedly the Assyrians, who introduced a bold large-scale art that glorified kingship and victory. The sun-dried brick buildings of Sumer have crumbled to dusty mounds, whereas remains of the Assyrians' stone palace-cities leave us in little doubt about their character and tastes. Most impressive of all are their reliefs, carved on a large scale to stand out from walls and other surfaces. They celebrate the glory of Sennacherib, Assurbanipal and other kings with vigorous, barbaric scenes in which the enemy hosts are destroyed, or enslaved and led off in triumph.

Halfway between sculpture 'in the round' and relief are the great Assyrian winged bulls with human heads, whose massive forms can be seen at the British Museum in London, for instance. They are copied by another imperial people, the Persians, for the entrance to Persepolis [10], a great stone city whose ruins commemorate an empire that stretched across the Middle East and down into Egypt. But, as the winged bulls show, Persian art was softer and less openly aggressive than the art of the Assyrians. It was something of a mixture of Assyrian, Greek and Egyptian elements, and can be said to end the ancient Mesopotamian tradition—but not before Mesopotamian artists had influenced the Hittites in Anatolia, the peoples of Syria and Palestine, and even the Nomads of Eurasia.

8

9

8 Helmet of Meskalamdug from Ur. Iraq Museum, Baghdad.

9 Bust of a bearded priest from the Indus Valley. Central Asian Antiquities Museum, New Delhi.

10 View of Persepolis from the Gate-House of Xerxes.

11

12

14

An interesting offshoot of Sumerian culture flourished around 2000 BC in the valley of the Indus River (now part of Pakistan) until it was destroyed some five hundred years later by Aryan invaders from Iran. A small stone bust of a man [9] is one of the finest works from this Indus Valley culture. It has a strange sad humanity despite the simplified way in which the face and beard have been carved. The artist seems to have given more conscious attention to the ornaments on the forehead, arm and torso, symbols of wealth and rank that were perhaps what the sitter cared about most.

Many people have the impression that Egyptian civilisation was the oldest in the world, though in fact it started a few hundreds years after Sumer, in about 3200 BC. The reason for this impression is that, unlike Mesopotamia, Egypt was remarkably stable, enduring for almost three thousand years under a divine ruler, the Pharaoh. Until its conquest by Persia in 525 BC, foreign occupations of Egypt were short-lived, and foreign influences few and weak enough to be easily assimilated. This also explains the uniformity of Egyptian art. It did change from one period to the next, but so little that only real experts can spot the differences. There was no challenge to the strict but quite satisfactory conventions which governed it—so that, for example, human beings are almost always shown in paintings and reliefs with eyes and torso seen from the front, and face and feet in profile.

The impression of changelessness and endurance is strengthened by the Egyptians' preoccupation with eternity, expressed in monumental terms, preferably in stone—in commemorative obelisks, colossal statues and temples, in the pyramids and the Great Sphinx. Belief in an afterlife—for which careful preparation was essential—led to the creation of an elaborate tomb art, thanks to which thousands of wall-paintings and decorative objects have been preserved; the most

11 King Mycerinus and Queen Chamerernebti. Museum of Fine Arts, Boston.

12. Head of Nefertiti. Egyptian Museum, West Berlin.

13 Columned hall at Karnak.

14 Detail from a 'Book of the Dead'. Egyptian Museum, Turin.

13

14

complete and lavish example is the famous tomb of Tutankhamun, discovered almost intact in 1922 with wonderful furnishings of gilded and carved wood, ivory and alabaster. Even the pyramids are just huge mausoleums, containing the tombs of the Pharaohs.

Not surprisingly, the most important Egyptian arts are the most monumental and least perishable: architecture and sculpture. And sculpture was, for all its quantity and size, only an auxiliary of architecture. Every sculptor designed his work to be viewed from the front – that is, he thought of it as part of a wall or as backing on to a wall; the body is shown not in action but upright, with arms and shoulders thrust back. We can see this 'frontal' quality even in the touching and domestic double portrait of Mycerinus and his Queen [11]: the Queen's hand, resting tenderly on her husband's body, comes straight out of a plain surface.

Egyptian statues generally make us more conscious of the subject's rank than of his personality: he is god-king or official personified, not an individual. The full portrait, reproducing specific characteristics, was made in only one brief period of Egyptian history. This artistic revolution accompanied the religious revolution begun by the Pharaoh Akhnaton, who favoured the worship of a single sun-god, Aton, and persecuted

followers of the other gods. Perhaps the two revolutions were not directly connected: as we shall also notice later in a Christian context, when men see the world in a different light, the difference appears in their art without their having consciously new artistic intentions. Akhnaton's queen, Nefertiti, the partner in his religious reforms, can be seen with him in double portraits and family groups, as well as in ceremonial settings. This portrait bust of Nefertiti [12] is one of the most famous of all ancient works of art, no doubt somewhat idealised, but womanly and informal, with long graceful neck, regular features and natural colouring – 'the most beautiful woman in Antiquity', as enthusiasts have called her.

The Egyptians built in stone to worship the gods and preserve the dead. Temples and tombs have survived, assembled by the labour of thousands or cut from living rock; palaces and homes have vanished. The greatest of all Egyptian temples are the linked temples of Amon at Luxor and Karnak, on the Nile – groups of huge horizontal buildings, the flat stone roofs supported by forests of columns.

The hall at Karnak [13] must have been a dim-lit awesome place, with its massive columns covered with hieroglyphics and living forms – a suitably intimidating and inspiring approach to the dark inner sanctum of the god.

The whole human journey – life, death and life-after-death – appears in Egyptian paintings on tombs and papyrus rolls. These often include all sorts of interesting details of everyday life, and show an unexpected delight in plants, birds, beasts and insects. The example here is from the rolls of the *Book of the Dead* [14], which was placed in the dead man's sarcophagus and contained all the information he needed to win acceptance in the afterlife; it links life and death – the pomp of a funerary voyage by water, with the humble round of work in the fields.

Civilisation in China began very much later (around 1500 BC), but once established it developed continuously down to modern times. The earliest dynasties were the Shang and the Chou, which together lasted about eleven centuries. Their art is magical and intense, markedly different from the later Chinese art – cool, formal, delicate – with which most people are familiar. Here too the emphasis is on magic and religion: archaeologists have dug up many objects used in ceremonial ancestor-worship – bones for divination, jade amulets, and magnificent bronze vessels that held offerings of food and drink. The Chinese craftsman gave his bronzes special magical powers by adding symbolic decorations that look completely abstract. In fact these make up a pattern of animal forms that have been fused together and simplified beyond recognition. The Shang vessel here [15], typically heavy and slightly sinister, shows what intricate beauty could be created by this transforming power of the imagination.

The Civilisation of Greece and Rome

In Near Eastern art we are never far away from the presence of gods and god-like kings; ordinary men and women appear mainly as regimented figures on friezes and tombs. The first civilised art of which man himself is the hero was created in the eastern Mediterranean, on the island of Crete and later on the Greek mainland.

Crete was a great sea-power, and her civilisation—called Minoan, after the King Minos of Greek mythology—was solidly based on trade. There were several great palaces and cities on the island, including the so-called palace of Minos at Knossos. The view of the royal apartments seen here [16] conveys a feeling of private and pleasurable living.

When the Minoan civilisation was destroyed by wars and earthquakes (about 1400 BC), its art was carried on by a Greek mainland people at Mycenae. Hardly anything remains of Mycenean culture except walled fortresses at Mycenae itself and at Tiryns, and some chamber tombs made from huge blocks of uncemented stone which are more like megalithic structures than Minoan buildings.

Renewed invasions by Greek-speaking peoples led to the destruction of the Mycenean culture by about 1100 BC. Out of the chaos that followed, there gradually emerged a number of small states, each with a city such as Athens, Corinth or Sparta as its nucleus. These tiny states forged the high culture of ancient Greece.

To most of us Greek art means perfection of the human form in sculpture and perfection of proportion in architecture. That is true, but it is not the whole truth. The Greeks' intentions changed over the centuries, and it is easier to appreciate the range of their achievement if we divide the history of Greek art into three periods—Archaic, Classical and Hellenistic—and look at each in turn.

Greek buildings, like those of Egypt, basically consist of stone roofs supported by columns. The familiar Greek temple, with its colonnade, cornice and triangular pediment, developed in Archaic Greece. The first form it took is called the Doric 'order' [17], which can be identified by the simple cushion capital. The whole design of a Greek building was based on a carefully worked-out theory of proportion that was elaborated with mathematical exactness.

As in earlier civilisations, the Greeks decorated their temples with statues of the gods; but their gods are images of the human form. This Archaic *kouros* [18] (statue of a young man or god) is probably the god Apollo. If we compare it with the Egyptian statue of King Mycerinus [11], we can see that the Greek sculptor made his work just as dignified, but was not content to 'stylise' its body: his god consists of human muscle and bone. Physical beauty is not yet idealised: the artist has just animated a traditional formula.

16 Palace of Knossos, Crete.

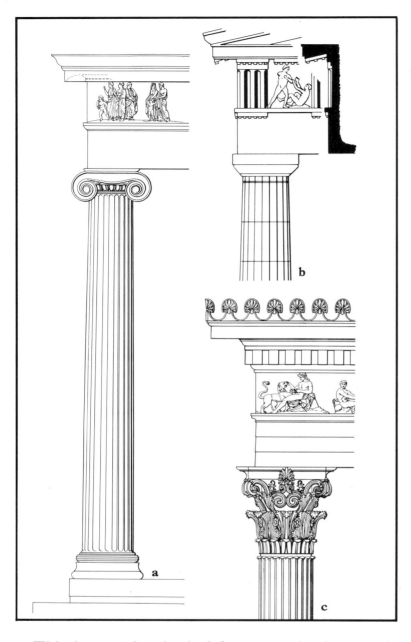

17 The three orders of architecture:
(a) Ionic column from temple on the Illissus, Athens.
(b) Doric capital from the Theseiou, Athens.
(c) Corinthian capital from the Choragic Monument of Lysicrates, Athens.

18 Bronze 'kouros' from Piraeus. National Archaeological Museum, Athens.

19 Exekias: Attic black-figure vase. British Museum, London.

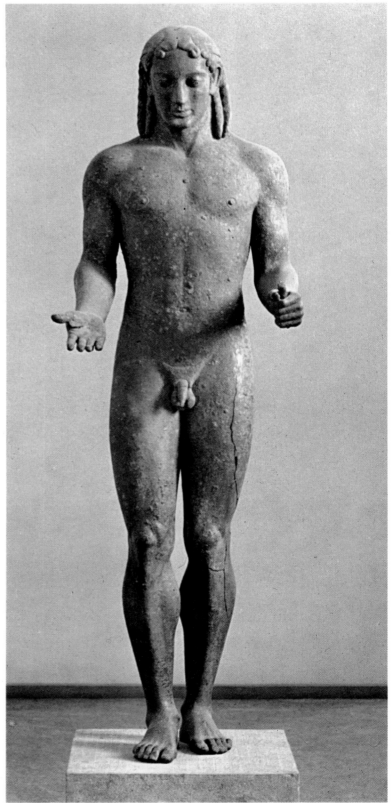

This interest in physical form can also be seen in Greek pottery painting, which developed into an important industry during the Archaic period. The rich mythology of the gods, stories from epic poetry, and scenes from contemporary life were recorded by painters on thousands of jars, bowls, cups and dishes. Corinth and, later, Athens were the centres of the 'black-figure' style, so called because the figures were painted in black straight on to the untouched earthenware surface. Details of anatomy and dress were added by scratching through the black paint into the earthenware. The picture might then be touched up with a few colours, such as the white and purple of Achilles slaying the Amazon queen Penthesilea, by the great Athenian master Exekias [19]. The 'red-figure' style, introduced late in the 6th century, was a great technical advance. The black-figure process was now reversed: the background was painted black, leaving the figures in the red of the earthenware, with an obvious gain in realistic effect.

The intellectual and artistic centre of Greece was Athens, which was also a great commercial power. Here

20 The Parthenon, Athens.

21 The Athena Group from the frieze of the Great Altar at Pergamon. Pergamon Museum, East Berlin.

22 Myron: The Discobolus (Roman copy of the Greek original). Terme Museum, Rome.

23 The Venus de Milo. Louvre, Paris.

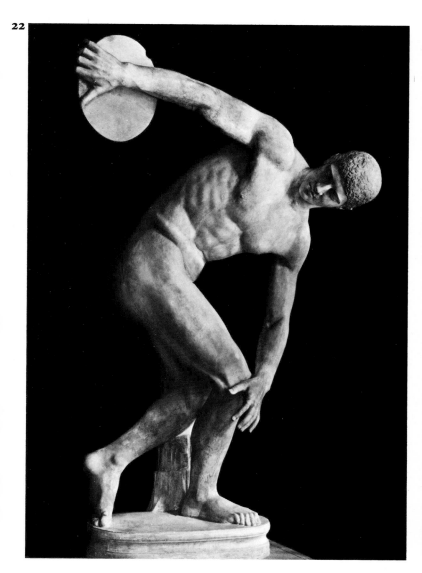

architects and artists, given opportunities to work on ambitious projects, produced works of profound creative imagination. The century between about 500 and 400 BC is known as the Classical period, when the Greeks achieved the ideal forms and perfect proportions mentioned earlier.

The greatest architectural project was the rebuilding of the Athenian acropolis, the hill fortress and civic-religious centre of the city. Dominating the hill is the temple of Athena Parthenos, better known as the Parthenon [20]. The Parthenon is the supreme expression of the Doric style; no other Doric building approaches the grandeur and refinement that make it one of the world's most famous buildings.

Myron's *Discobolus* (Discus Thrower), seen here [22] in a Roman marble copy of the bronze, shows how completely Classical sculptors broke with the past. Myron set himself to show harmonious athletic movement. His choice of the posture and proportions of the nude figure achieves the Greek ideal of athletic beauty, conveying the tension of the body in action, in what is in fact not a realistic pose.

The Peloponnesian War at the end of the 5th century destroyed the supremacy of Athens, and with it the Classical ideal. The next generation of artists claimed greater freedom of expression. The temples that were

now built on the Acropolis, the Erechtheion and the temple of the Wingless Victory, are early examples of a new style imported from the Greek cities of Asia Minor, the graceful and more decorated Ionic [17].

The innovating spirit in sculpture was heralded by Praxiteles, who in about 350 BC sculpted the first female nudes—a subject that has inspired artists ever since. Praxiteles' works are more soft and gentle in outline than Classical sculptures, and this tendency became still more pronounced during the subsequent Hellenistic period.

The sort of intense dramatic situations found in Hellenistic art can be seen on this fragment of a frieze from Pergamon [21], in which the battle between gods and giants comes over as a real matter of life and death. A strong taste for luxury and decoration also appeared. The new Corinthian order of architecture [17], with its flamboyant acanthus-leaf capitals, was often used in conjunction with the Ionic order – a disregard for pure form that would have horrified earlier generations.

Some of the best-known Greek statues date from the Hellenistic age. The most famous now is the Venus de Milo [23], which was discovered on the island of Melos in 1820. Her relaxed pose and unemotional expression look back 250 years to the days of Praxiteles, and reveal the respect still felt for the older ideals.

The Romans, who were emerging as a Mediterranean power when the Venus de Milo was being made, also showed great respect for Greek art. They had already been impressed by what they had seen in the Greek cities of southern Italy, and even as they took over the Greek lands in the Near East they became patrons of Greek artists and avid collectors of Greek antiquities. But they also had separate artistic traditions, especially in architecture and portrait sculpture, which were to have a great influence on later European art.

Roman building methods represented a great technical advance. They invented a powerful mortar which they faced with brick or marble; and they developed and made brilliant use of the arch, the vault and the dome. These engineering devices enabled them to roof large interiors and radically to change the appearance and function of buildings. Hence their theatres and amphitheatres, domed temples, triumphal arches, public baths and aqueducts, which dwarfed earlier Greek buildings. The Colosseum in Rome [24] is a magnificent example of a Roman amphitheatre. It is four storeys high, and the auditorium, which rests on great concrete vaults, can hold 45,000 people. The only Greek features are the decorative details – engaged columns (i.e. attached to the walls) with Doric, Ionic and Corinthian capitals, superimposed on the first three storeys. This irreverent use of the Greek orders was copied in a dutifully antiquarian spirit by Renaissance and later architects.

The most original and characteristic Roman sculptures are commemorative portraits and narrative reliefs. The tradition of portraiture was taken over from the Etruscans, a people who were a power in Italy before the Romans, and whose culture is still partly wrapped in mystery. Some Roman portraits are idealised in a noble, heroic, Greek manner, but the ones we tend to find more striking are those in which the

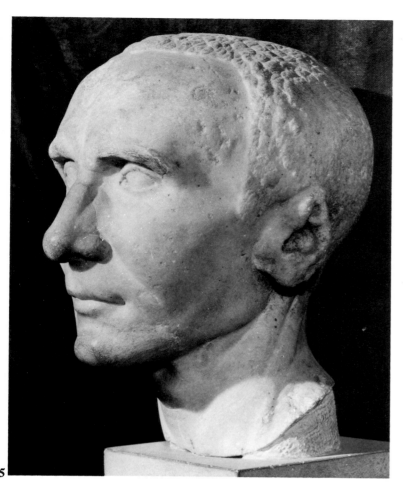

individual's personality is revealed, like this straightforward portrait of an unknown Roman citizen [25].

A good many delightful Roman wall paintings have survived, especially from Pompeii and Herculaneum, where they were partly preserved under layers of volcanic ash. Many of them decorated private houses; it is interesting to notice that in the privacy of his own home a Roman liked to surround himself with landscape and theatrical subjects, and stories from popular myths and legends. Mosaics—pictures made up of hundreds of small coloured stones—were a very practical way of decorating the home. They have been preserved in every corner of the Roman Empire, from Hadrian's Wall on the Scottish border to Morocco and the Lebanon. The finest are those in North Africa, like this imaginative procession of sea maidens and sea monsters [26].

The traditions of Roman art decayed along with the values that inspired them. Even before the Barbarian invasions there was a mood of discouragement and pessimism that led men to turn from the physical to the spiritual and other-worldly. The climax of this movement came in the 4th century AD, when Christianity was established as the religion of the Roman state, promising salvation in the life to come—a revaluation of man's destiny that in time produced a quite different art.

24 The Colosseum, Rome.

25 Head of an unknown Roman. Louvre, Paris.

26 Nereids and sea-monsters. Mosaic from Lambaesis, Algeria. Municipal Museum, Lambaesis.

Hindu and Buddhist India

About 1500 BC Aryan tribesmen entered India by the passes of the north-west, destroyed the Indus Valley culture, and drove the Dravidian inhabitants into the south of the peninsula. The invaders brought with them the Vedic religion–from which modern Hinduism has evolved–but no art. They appear to have distrusted images as idolatrous, an attitude shared at various times by peoples of other religions, including Christians and Muslims. At any rate, a revival of artistic activity occurred only in the 3rd century BC, and in connection with a relatively new religion, Buddhism. Persian influences–possibly even Persian craftsmen, fleeing from the conquering armies of Alexander the Great– may also have been at work.

The Indian temperament seems to be drawn to the most physically tangible of the arts–sculpture–and to an opulence and sensuality that was only partly suppressed by Buddhist austerity: the seductive, cheerful *yakshi* [**27**] were tree-nymphs, taken over into Buddhism from an older fertility-cult and evidently welcomed with ardour. This taste is in contrast to the Classical Greek preference for the athletic male figure: the Indian sculptor found satisfaction in ripeness and growth, the Greek in defined and proportioned forms.

The school of Mathura, which produced the *yakshi*, was renowned for sculptures of the female form. At roughly the same time, at Amaravati in the south, a school of carving was working in a less robust but attractively sinuous style. A third contemporary school was that of Gandhara. This was in the north-west–still the gateway to India–and came under the influence of Greek art, transmitted via Persia, an influence so powerful that the resulting Indian style is known as 'Greco-Buddhist' or 'Indo-Greek'. Artists were now permitted to represent the Buddha, and the Gandhara version [**28**] is truly 'Indo-Greek', with Westernised features and a head that blends religious serenity with a Classical nobility.

The surviving architecture of this and subsequent periods is entirely religious. The *stupa*, a building intended to house relics, was at first a balustraded structure with a flattened dome; later it developed into a pyramid-shape. Other Buddhist structures, the temple-sanctuary and the monastery or *vihara*, are remarkable in having been cut from the living rock– true to Indian taste, as much like sculpture as architecture. The temple at Ajanta [**30**] gives the impression of being organic rather than man-made, struggling to

27 Yakshi on a balustrade from Mathura. Indian Museum, Calcutta.

28 Buddha preaching (detail). Gandhara school. Indian Museum, Calcutta.

29 The mandapa at Srirangam.

maintain itself against the encroaching rock. It was built in the Gupta period (4th–6th centuries AD), when most of India was united under the Gupta dynasty, and music and literature flourished side by side with the visual arts. The sculptural style still owed a great deal to Greek art, though modified by Mathura roundness and increasingly inward and spiritual in expression.

The Hindu attitude towards life, with its powerful sense of creation—of abundance, proliferation, diversity —further emphasised the organic quality of Indian art. During the medieval period, thousands of temples were built all over the sub-continent, and covered— overrun—with dense armies of carved figures. These, whether in relief or (much more rarely) in the round, were more than ever fused with the architecture. Look at the figures from the 15th-century Horse Court at Srirangam [29]. Where decoration ends and structure begins is almost impossible to say.

By this time temples were free-standing structures, but still essentially sculptural—piles or imitation mountains, built up in tiers and swarming with living things. The concealment of structure and blurring of outlines— apparent too in the circular flowing compositions on the walls at Ajanta, unframed and without beginning or end—seem to be integral elements of Indian taste; the Gandhara-Gupta phase, splendid as it is, can be regarded as an alien 'Greek' intrusion.

30

31

The kind of restrained purity of line associated with Buddhism is found only in the Dravidian south. Quantities of magnificent sculptures were produced here throughout the Middle Ages and into the Muslim period. Unlike the stone sculptures of the north, they are all in the round, and were often carried in processions. Shiva dancing [32] was a particularly popular subject.

Missionaries and traders spread the influence of Indian art in central and south-east Asia. In Indonesia the most interesting works come from Java; the 9th-century *stupa* at Barabudur is one of the greatest achievements of Buddhist art, an amazing terraced mountain-pyramid decorated with tender stylised reliefs. The Khmer people of Cambodia produced a Hindu art of independent interest, at its height during the 10th–12th centuries. Its climax was the great temple of Angkor Wat [31], a huge moated complex, superbly planned and decorated, which served as temple, palace and mausoleum for the Khmer god-king. This is a masterpiece of world architecture, surpassing anything built in India itself.

30 Façade of Cave 19, Ajanta.
31 Angkor Wat, Cambodia.
32 Shiva dancing. Rijksmuseum, Amsterdam.

32

The Climax of Chinese Art

In 221 BC, after years of ruthless warfare, the Chinese states were united under a single emperor, Cheng, founder of the Ch'in dynasty; from 'Ch'in' comes our word 'China'. Over the next 2000-odd years the political history of the empire followed a recurrent pattern: early unity and strength under capable rulers, a period of gradual decline under their decadent successors, and finally disintegration, often through invasions by nomadic peoples from the north. Several of the dynasties ruled for such long periods that they marked distinct epochs in Chinese history; and therefore it is worth examining Chinese art and society in dynastic terms.

The Ch'in were soon succeeded by the Han (206 BC–AD 220), whose organisation of the state partly determined the development of Chinese society. The highly efficient and cultivated civil service was composed of successful examination candidates who had studied the thoughts of Confucius and his followers. The Confucian emphasis on right conduct, and its conservative cult of reverence for ancestors, shaped the outlook of the administrative class. These 'literati' patronised and also practised the arts. They created Chinese poetry, music, scroll-painting and calligraphy, and their tastes largely determined the kind of works produced by potters, sculptors and architects. Chinese art, with its avoidance of violence, disorder and extreme emotion, owes much of its distinctive character to the Confucian bureaucrat.

Han art survives mainly in the form of tomb-furnishings – quantities of jewellery, cosmetics, clothes, utensils and other household goods, all made, as in Egypt, for the use of the dead man in the afterlife. Pottery models of desirable objects, and of men, dogs and horses, replaced the real creatures sacrificed in less civilised times, and are among the most attractive items. The toilet box shown here [34] is an example of the luxury art of lacquering, which flourished in Han times. Lacquer is the resin of a tree and, after being boiled, is applied in many successive layers to wood or, as here, to hemp. The box is decorated with animals and abstract patterns, and with silver inlays, of which a mounted archer is visible in the illustration. Silk is often found in the tombs; the secret of its manufacture was known only to the Chinese, and the Silk Route across central Asia brought Han China into contact with imperial Rome.

33

33 Bodhisattva. Museum of Fine Arts, Boston (Gift of Denman Waldo Ross in memory of Okakura Kakuzo).

34 Toilet box. Han period. British Museum, London.

35 Horse of unglazed pottery. T'ang dynasty. Ashmolean Museum, Oxford.

37

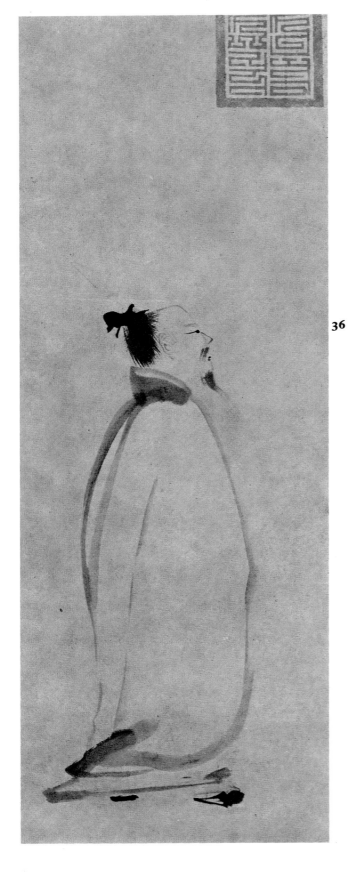

36

The next period, the Six Dynasties (AD 220–618), was one of disintegration. There was a tendency for Confucianism, with its strong ethical bent, to give way to religions with deeper emotional appeal, more satisfying in times of stress: Taoism in the south, Buddhism in the north, where a number of Barbarian states had been set up. With Buddhism came rock-cut temples and their lavish sculptures and wall-paintings; but Chinese culture was already too well-established to be simply swamped by Indian art. The lifesize Bodhisattva [33] (incarnation of the Buddha) shows how successfully Chinese sculptors adopted and adapted Buddhist subjects and artistic conventions. The narrow figure and stylised features are a world away from the naturalism of Indian Buddhist art; the alien influence is most striking in the Bodhisattva's smile–for the Chinese face is shown smiling only in the Six Dynasties period. Another import from India was the pagoda, with its tapering series of roofs, a Chinese elaboration of the Indian *stupa*. The status of painting changed in this period: previously an art for the masses in the form of edifying wall-paintings, it was now also taken up by the *literati*, who worked on silk or paper scrolls which were intended to be gradually unrolled and scrutinised at leisure by the connoisseur.

Reunited under the Sui dynasty, the Chinese empire reached its greatest extent under the T'ang (618–906). Their conquests in central Asia opened the way for renewed influences from India, and from Sassanian Persia and lands still further west. These help to explain the realism of T'ang art – a feature at variance with the main tendency of Chinese art, in which there is almost always some degree of deliberate stylisation. Grave-goods are again the most impressive surviving objects, as sophisticated as their Han counterparts, but also virile and lifelike. Pottery figures were made both with and without glazes (coatings of glassy material); the war-horse here [35] is a typical unglazed work, a masterpiece of tension and vigour. A vast amount of Buddhist art must have been created, but most of it disappeared in the persecutions of the 9th century which effectively destroyed the power of the Buddhists.

The break-up of the T'ang state was followed by a period of chaos from which emerged a new imperial dynasty, the Sung (960–1279). This was the last great creative period of Chinese art, and much Sung work already displays an over-refinement that is charming but suggestive of exhausted vitality. Appreciation grew – or at least was institutionalised – as creativity declined: an academy of painting was founded, great collections were built up, and sophisticated theories were developed. Still, Sung painting is wonderfully delicate and atmospheric, though perhaps escapist in its penchant for misty, impressionistic landscapes in which man is either absent or tiny and insignificant.

An alternative tradition of painting was associated with Zen Buddhism, which emphasised immediacy of experience and intuition: ink paintings done in a graphic style with a few rapid brushstrokes. Here we see the great T'ang poet Li Po [36], who celebrated the enchantments of wine, love and the moon; the Sung painter gives us a purified image of the hard-drinking bard, presenting him as a wanderer or contemplative. This style of ink painting, along with Zen itself, was to be exported to Japan, where it was enthusiastically practised.

The art of making pottery vases, jars and bottles was highly developed as early as the T'ang period. Chinese craftsmen used glazes and decorations in several colours, and evolved the three main types of pottery – which are, in ascending order of hardness, earthenware, stoneware and porcelain. Though lacking the vigour of T'ang ware, Sung works are unsurpassed for their subtle, refined shapes and cool decoration; to many tastes they are the supreme achievement of Chinese art. This stoneware vase [37] is a deeply satisfying piece with a purity of line that entices the eye up and down the length of its body and neck; the mottled colours, elegant and quiet, reinforce the impression of serene, finished, untroubled beauty.

During the Yuan period (1260–1368), China was incorporated in the great Mongol empire, which stretched over most of Asia and European Russia. The Mongols set themselves to learn from the civilisation they had conquered, although under their influence a more realistic spirit again appeared in Chinese art. As if in reaction, a new style of painting was introduced by Huang Kung-wang [38], an ex-official and Taoist priest who retired to the hills. He spent the rest of his life painting landscapes, with a Chinese delicacy but in a new manner, at once sharp and sketchy, that was used by many later painters.

38

Byzantium and Christian Europe

The triumph of Christianity in the 4th century AD did not immediately revolutionise Roman art. In the west, Christian artists simply took over the Greco-Roman art forms and reinterpreted them in terms of the new religion—just as the Church took over pagan festivals held at Christmas and Easter. So, for example, conventional pictures of the life of Orpheus continued to be produced, but with Jesus substituted for the mythical hero. With the exception of a few symbols, the same is true of the wall-paintings in the famous catacombs, the underground cemeteries in which Christians buried their dead before Christianity became the state religion.

The churches which replaced the old pagan temples were also adaptations, in this case from the Roman basilica. The basilica was a civic building used for assemblies and markets—a rectangular hall with a large main area (the nave) and colonnaded passageways (the aisles). In the 5th-century basilica of Sant' Apollinare Nuovo [39], Ravenna, the position of the altar has become fixed at the far end, and a semicircular area, the apse, placed beyond it. In later churches additional areas extended to the right and left of the altar (the transepts), giving the church its traditional and symbolic cross-shape.

In the 5th century the Roman empire in the west collapsed under the impact of wave after wave of nomadic peoples—the 'Barbarians'—in search of refuge, land or loot. Visigoths, Ostrogoths, Vandals and others set up states in Italy, France, Spain and North Africa. The new rulers were generally anxious to understand and appropriate Roman civilisations, and quickly adopted its Christian religion; but the disruption of economic and political life inevitably led to a cruder culture and the loss of both technical and artistic skills. In the wealthy Greek east the Roman empire managed to cope with the Barbarian threat, and survived for another thousand years. Its capital, Constantinople, was long the greatest city in Christendom, and its old Greek name, Byzantium, is used to describe the whole empire.

Politically stable and geographically open to influences from the anti-realistic Middle East, this empire evolved a Christian art that owed little to the Greco-Roman tradition. To people brought up on 'photographic' art, Byzantine works look merely incompetent, whereas the truth is that the Byzantine artist had an unfamiliar aim—to convey a spiritual rather than a physical reality. For this reason he showed only those human features that had religious or symbolic meaning; made emperors and saints bigger

39

39 Interior of Sant' Apollinare Nuovo, Ravenna.

40 The Empress Theodora and her suite. Mosaic in San Vitale, Ravenna.

41 Sancta Sophia, Istanbul.

40

41

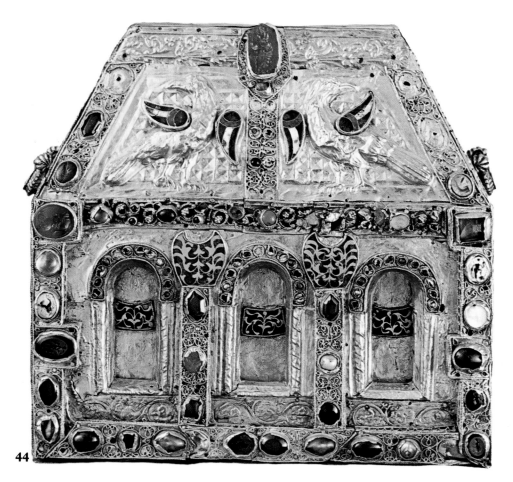

43

44

than other people in the same picture because they were more important; made little attempt to convey a sense of movement or bodily presence beneath clothing; and replaced landscape with a flat gold surface that put the pictured event in a timeless sphere outside profane history.

Many of these features are already visible in the 6th-century mosaics [40] of San Vitale at Ravenna. Ravenna was the chief Byzantine stronghold in Italy, won by the armies of the Emperor Justinian, who for a time seemed destined to drive the Barbarians from the west and recreate the Mediterranean empire of Rome. It is Justinian's greatness that is celebrated on the walls of San Vitale. The reproduction shows his Empress, Theodora, and her suite: despite the rigid frontal poses and the priest-like and mysterious air of the haloed sovereign, there is probably still an element of portraiture in the faces of the group. The choice of mosaic for this great work is significant. The preferred arts of Byzantium are the least three-dimensional: mosaic, which lends itself to brilliant colours and imposing formal effects rather than natural modelling; manuscript illumination—the art of illustrating and embellishing books; and low-relief carving on such materials as ivory, the figures hardly standing out at all from the surface. Nothing could be further away than this from the physical awareness of the Indian artist [27].

The characteristic Byzantine style in architecture evolved from a technical discovery: how to join a large round dome on to its square base. The great buildings in the style appeared soon after the problem had been

42 The Virgin of Vladimir. Tretyakov Gallery, Moscow.
43 Byzantine goblet. Treasury of St Mark's, Venice.
44 The Pepin Reliquary. Abbey treasury, Conques, France.

solved: San Vitale at Ravenna, St Sergius and St Bacchus at Constantinople, and Sancta Sophia, also at Constantinople. Sancta Sophia [41] was designed for Justinian by the architects Anthemius of Tralles and Isidorus of Miletus. It was intended as a deliberate assertion of imperial greatness, and is indeed one of the world's great buildings—a complex of mutually supporting domes and vaults with a huge high central dome or cupola. Since the fall of Constantinople to the Turks (1453), Sancta Sophia has been a mosque; the four Turkish minarets give the building a misleading though effective 'Eastern' appearance.

In the 7th century the Arabs conquered the North African and Middle Eastern possessions of Byzantium, and for a time it seemed that the whole empire might collapse. Arab influence was probably responsible for the subsequent 'iconoclast' crisis, which entailed the condemnation of all but abstract designs: to make an image (icon) of anything that existed was considered idolatrous by the iconoclasts ('icon-breakers'). In the 9th-century, under Basil II and his successors, Byzantium made a political recovery. At about the same time iconoclasm ended, and Byzantine art entered a new phase of achievement. It also spread—through the Balkans to Russia, and along the Mediterranean to Venice and Sicily. Mosaic retained its pre-eminence,

45 Title page of the Book of Kells. Trinity College Library, Dublin.

46 St Matthew. A page from the Ebbo Gospel. Bibliothèque Municipale, Epernay.

and some of the most awe-inspiring works of the post-iconoclast period are the figures of Christ Pantocrator (Almighty), stern judge of sinners, gazing down on the congregation from the ceilings of church domes. Wall-paintings were also produced, often imbued with an emotional intensity new in Byzantine art. Shown here [42] is a famous icon−a small religious painting on wood− which conveys a painful, brooding compassion, as if the Virgin is suffering in the foreknowledge of her Child's Crucifixion. This, *Our Lady of Vladimir*, was painted in Constantinople but taken to Russia, where it provided the model for an iconic tradition that lasted down to recent times.

Throughout Byzantine history its craftsmen produced exquisite luxury objects, using precious metals and stones, ivory, enamels and textiles. This goblet [43] is a 12th-century work in which the glowing transparent glass is set off by the elaborate gold work encrusted with enamels and precious stones.

A comparison of the goblet with the heavily magnificent Pepin reliquary [44] reveals the gulf between the civilised refinement of Byzantium and the crude energy of the Franks, who were then engaged in building an empire in western Europe. Reliquaries were containers used in the Christian world to hold the relics of saints. Clearly it was essential to emphasise the

veneration in which a saint was held by making the reliquary as sumptuous as possible. Gold, jewels, enamels, ivory and other rare and precious materials were used in their construction, and the finest available craftsmanship was lavished on them. Often a reliquary was made in the shape of a church [60], the 'house of God', to make sure that God as well as the saint inhabited the reliquary. The Pepin reliquary is made of wood covered with beaten and worked gold; again, enamels and precious stones enhance the effect of richness. Metalwork with ornamental and animal designs (notice the eagles on the lid of the reliquary) was a Barbarian contribution to European art. The taste for elaborate abstract ornament appears even more strongly in the school of manuscript illumination that flourished in Celtic Ireland and Anglo-Saxon England, reaching its peak in 8th-century Northumbria. In the Lindisfarne Gospel, and to an even greater degree in the Book of Kells, the human figure is absorbed into a larger decorative pattern. The most impressive and satisfying pages are those such as the one here [45], in which a single letter grows like an exotic plant into a mass of intricate ornament.

The establishment of a Frankish empire was followed by the coronation of the Frankish King Charlemagne as Holy Roman Emperor. This event, which took place in Rome in the year 800, was the first step out of the Dark Ages. The new empire was not in fact Roman or even Mediterranean, but north European−a decisive cultural shift; but, not for the first time, Europeans found it convenient to define themselves by reference back to Antiquity. Conscious of inheriting the Roman purple, Charlemagne was an enthusiast for the arts, and the 'Caroligian renaissance' owed a great deal to imperial patronage. Interest in representation revived, largely thanks to contact with the art of early Christian Rome and, to a lesser extent, Byzantium. Manuscript illumination was the most flourishing art, practised in the monasteries that were being founded all over the empire. Styles varied widely. One of the most interesting is that of the Gospel Book of Ebbo; in one illumination [46], the frenzied lines of St Matthew's robe, his wild hair and the sketched-in landscape behind him express the saint's high emotion as he writes his life of Jesus−and perhaps too a monkish appreciation of the pains of authorship. Architecture was equally diverse. Roman elements were incorporated in some buildings, while the palace chapel at Charlemagne's capital, Aachen, was built in direct imitation of the Byzantine church of San Vitale at Ravenna. Finally Barbarian and Celtic influence remained strong in ornament. In other words, the Caroligian renaissance did not introduce a new style; it represents the (only half-successful) attempt of a young, crude and vigorous society to absorb and put to use everything that came to hand. In doing so it laid a basis for the great styles of the European Middle Ages.

The World of Islam

Whereas the West struggled for centuries to achieve some kind of stability, the dynamic new Arabian religion of Islam created a powerful civilisation in little more than a hundred years. In AD 630 the troops of Muhammad, prophet of the new faith, gained their first great victory by capturing Mecca. Soon they controlled the whole of Arabia; and in the next thirty years they conquered Persia, Mesopotamia and Egypt. By 750 Islam held sway from Spain and North Africa in the west to the borders of China in the east.

Like the Roman Empire, Islam brought unity to half the known world. The art to which it gave birth was also essentially a unity, despite the existence of local styles; and it remained so even when the empire broke up into a number of smaller and often mutually hostile states. It is above all an art of intricate pattern and brilliant colour, used to create superbly decorated surfaces: building surfaces of carved or pierced stone, coloured marble and painted tiles; of gleaming painted pottery, elaborately wrought metalwork, and rich textiles and carpets. Everywhere we find a wealth of pattern created out of geometrical and living forms. The Muslim artist makes a design, not a picture of things or events, as if preoccupied with the infinite rather than the material world or the passing moment.

Islamic 'anti-naturalism' has led people to think— wrongly—that Muslim artists were not allowed to represent living things. In fact they could and often did— though never on mosques, where images of the real might tempt believers into idolatry. The impulse to pattern went much deeper than prohibitions: the artist used images, but nearly always stylised them and worked them into an all-encompassing surface decoration in which any reference to reality was lost. From the Greco-Roman tradition he took models drawn from nature— vines, leaves, scrolls—and transformed them into lacy 'arabesque' patterns. He used patterns of lines to form abstract elements such as stars and polygons. And he even made patterns from Arabic writing, so that quotations from the Koran became pure decoration.

Pattern, not structure, strikes the eye at once in the interior of the great mosque at Cordoba [47]. In a medieval Christian church, the arches are very obviously supportive; here, their double form, slender supports and two-colour scheme emphasise the relationship between arch and arch instead of between arch and roof. The coloured bricks also serve to draw the eye down the length of the hall, apparently endless beneath receding arches.

From the 9th century the Turkish peoples of central Asia began to play an important part in the history of Islam. One of these, the Seljuks, eventually took Baghdad and became the greatest power in the Middle East. The Seljuks excelled at pottery, and made glowing painted earthenware tiles a major feature of Islamic building, enriching interiors and making the domes of Islamic buildings one of the world's most dazzling and brilliant sights. Seljuk pots were carved, moulded, glazed, and decorated with either naturalistic or completely abstract designs. A Muslim speciality was lustreware, pottery painted with special pigments that gave the surface a gleaming metallic appearance. It was practised by the Seljuks, who learned it from Islamic Egypt, which flourished between the 10th and 12th centuries under the Fatimid dynasty. The illustration [48] is of a plate from Kashan in Persia, with figures, plants and dense decoration superbly designed to fit within the border of Persian poetry. The great Islamic tradition of rug- and carpet-making was also the contribution of the Seljuks.

A more violent irruption was made in the 13th century by the Mongols, already noticed as conquerors of China. They overran Persia and the rest of the Middle East, destroying cities and shaking Islamic society before being converted and accepting much of the culture of the conquered. Incorporation into the vast Mongol empire brought Islam into closer contact with the Far East, and particularly affected the development of the miniatures painted to illustrate books—perhaps the outstanding Muslim art in which human and animal figures are freely used.

47

Hardly more than a hundred years later, a new Turkish conqueror descended from central Asia: Timur, or Tamerlaine. One of the best-preserved Timurid buildings is the mausoleum [49] in which the conqueror and his family lie, its massy, rather forbidding forms lightened by geometrical and calligraphic decoration, and set off by the magnificent ridged dome of turquoise tiles.

Although built at roughly the same time, the Lion Court [51] has the elegance that comes of long sophistication. It is part of the famous Alhambra Palace at Granada, and blends the natural and the highly artificial in perfect harmony.

At the other end of the Islamic world, Persia became a great power under the Safavid dynasty (about 1500–1720). Isfahan became the Safavid capital under Shah Abbas, and he and his successors built the Masjid-i

Shah and many other buildings that have made the city famous. Interiors were of an unparalleled intensity of colouring, and a nebulous other-worldliness created by architectural devices such as tiled 'stalactites' hanging from the ceilings. Books became works of visual art, the Safavid miniature being complemented by fine binding and exquisite calligraphy. At the same time the miniature assumed a new importance, evolving into a picture in its own right, independent of literary texts. The painting of Muhammad [50], riding through the heavens on a human-headed steed, was done in about 1540. True to Islamic tradition, it is a mass of colour and detail; but the artist has also succeeded in generating a sense of

47 The mosque at Cordoba.
48 Ceramic lustre plate made by Sayyid Shams al-din al Hasani. The Smithsonian Institution, Freer Gallery, Washington.

48

excitement and movement, with busy angels, flickering flames and swirling clouds.

The last Islamic empire was created by yet another Turkish people, the Ottomans, whose descendants still inhabit modern Turkey. The Ottomans conquered the Middle East, and in 1453 took Constantinople (modern Istanbul), bringing to a close the long history of the Byzantine empire. They burst into the Balkans and threatened the very existence of Christian Europe. As late as 1683 they were able to lay siege to Vienna, and although their empire afterwards steadily declined, it did not collapse until the Great War of 1914–18.

The fall of Constantinople has one curious sequel: Justinian's Sancta Sophia so impressed the Turks that they transformed it into a mosque, and also copied and developed its central dome plan for their own mosques. The ironical result is that all over the Middle East the traveller can find Muslim architecture derived from a great Christian building of fourteen hundred years ago.

The Turkish carpet shows the enduring Muslim feeling for design. Persian carpets were sometimes made with hunting scenes and other figures, but Turkish carpets were always either abstract or floral, in a limited range of colours, drawing on centuries-old traditions of weaving, knotting and design in Turkish central Asia. Carpets with purely abstract linear designs are called 'Holbein' [52] in the West because they appear in paintings by the 16th-century German artist Holbein; Europeans valued them so highly that they placed them not on floors but on tables and walls.

49

49 Timur's Mausoleum, Samarkand.

50 Manuscript painting by Sultan Muhammad from a copy of Nizami's Khamsa. British Museum, London.

51 The Lion Court in the Alhambra, Granada.

52 'Holbein' carpet from Turkey. Gift of Joseph V. McMullan, 1961, Metropolitan Museum of Art, New York.

The Middle Ages

53 Isaiah. Abbey church, Souillac.
54 Ste Foy, Conques.

The stability provided by the Caroligian empire hardly survived its founder, Charlemagne. In the centuries that followed, Christian Europe often seemed likely to collapse under the blows of new enemies: the Muslim Arabs, the Vikings, and the Magyar nomads who eventually settled down in Hungary. Only in the 11th century were some of the pressures relaxed.

The Church prospered: even the most ruthless robber-baron tried to secure a place in Paradise by founding a monastery–which could then also be used to start a younger son or nephew on a clerical career. Less fortunate people tried to buy relics of saints, or went on pilgrimages to see and perhaps touch a famous relic. Far-away Jerusalem was the most meritorious goal, but most devout people contented themselves with a visit–still hazardous enough–to European shrines such as Santiago de Compostella in Spain.

The routes the pilgrims took were marked by some magnificent churches, mostly begun in the second half of the 11th century. The main source of inspiration for these was the Benedictine abbey at Cluny in France, which had begun a powerful movement to establish the Church as independent of all worldly authority. This new image–of an independent Church as leader of society and in charge of its own affairs–was projected by the new Romanesque art.

'Romanesque' is a modern label, used because the general features of the churches, and in particular the vaulting, owe so much to Roman example. The nave of the abbey church at Conques [54], with its heavy masonry and round arches, gives a good idea of the solid, impressive qualities of Romanesque buildings. Thick walls and massive pillars were necessary to take the strain of the vaults–usually, as here, tunnel or barrel vaults rather like a long continuous round arch. The style spread all over western Europe, and was brought to England by her Norman conquerors, so that English Romanesque is known as 'Norman'.

Romanesque sculpture consists almost entirely of architectural decoration such as the carved capitals of columns and reliefs above and around the doors of churches. Some are strongly expressive, using crude but vigorous grotesques to convey images of death and judgment, as at Autun in Burgundy. Others are more patterned and stylised, suggesting the influence of manuscript illumination and Byzantine art; the carver of the Isaiah at Souillac [53], for example, thought in

terms of elegant flowing lines rather than three-dimensional forms.

In the 12th century there was a European awakening as important as the better-known Italian Renaissance some three centuries later. The universities of Paris and Oxford became great centres of learning, Peter Abelard began a new era in Christian philosophy, and the Cistercian monk St Bernard of Clairvaux led a revival of religious enthusiasm. Bernard detested Cluniac pomp and display, and disapproved of the Roman-style round arches and heavy columns as smacking of a pagan past. He found his ideal—an austere, specifically Christian and contemporary art—in the rapidly evolving Gothic style.

Gothic was the first truly European style—European, not Roman or Byzantine, in spirit and technique. Like Romanesque it was developed first in France, now a wealthy land with a strong monarchy and independent towns. It was the towns that built the great Gothic cathedrals, which were civic as well as religious centres. Civic feeling was intensely competitive, driving each town in turn to put up a bigger and better cathedral

55 Interior of Cologne cathedral.

56 Stained glass in Chartres cathedral showing Charlemagne giving orders for the building of a church.

than the last. Notre Dame in Paris, Chartres, Reims, Amiens, were built progressively higher, until at Beauvais ambition outstripped engineering skill, and parts of the building collapsed.

Height and light are the dominant features of the cathedrals—soaring buildings whose walls have huge window areas that allow light to flood into the interior. Inside, as at Cologne [55], slim pillars rise unbroken from floor to ceiling, where pointed arches add to the vertical effect, so that the spirit too soars.

Several important engineering discoveries made it possible for architects to break with the heavy-walled, low-arched Romanesque style. The crossed ribs visible on the ceiling at Cologne concentrated the strain from the roof at a few points, so that massive carrying walls became unnecessary; the Gothic wall is a mere shell—a frame for expanses of glass. The pointed arch, really two separate segments that could meet at angles of varying steepness, gave far greater stability than the fixed semicircle of the round arch. And a new device, the flying buttress [57], supported the greater height without blocking up the windows with a mass of masonry piled against the walls. The flying buttress is a kind of permanent scaffolding supporting the building at one remove: the thrust is transferred to massive blocks at a distance by elegantly curving blades of stone.

The large window spaces of the cathedrals gave rise to a brilliant window-art. Stained glass is rather like mosaic in that it is made up of pieces of glass stained with metal oxides and joined together by leading; but it transmits light instead of reflecting it. A work like the Charlemagne window [56] is beautiful to look at; but when you turn away you are still bathed in its glowing colours, which heighten the impression that at Chartres you have stepped out of the world into a new reality. Gothic sculptors also broke decisively with Romanesque. The two column figures from Reims cathedral [58] immediately remind us of Classical Greek art: they are noble and serene, untouched by violence or high emotion. The drapery is not applied as ornament or used to express frenzy, but suggests the presence of real bodies beneath it.

The Gothic impulse from France was taken up in western Europe. In Germany the cathedrals of Cologne and Strasbourg, in Spain Burgos, Toledo and León, were all directly inspired by French examples.

Distinctive national traits did appear in other arts. In Germany the sufferings of Jesus on the Cross gave an outlet for northern emotionalism in expressive distorted woodcarvings like the *Pestkreuz* [59] in a church in Cologne. Here Christ is a skeletal creature with an exaggerated ribcage and claw-like hands and feet—a

57

58

59

57 Flying
buttress.
Chartres
cathedral.

58 The
Visitation.
Reims
cathedral.

59 German
Crucifixion
('Pestkreuz').
St Maria im
Kapitol,
Cologne.

60 Reliquary of gilded copper and walrus ivory. Kunstgewerbemuseum, West Berlin.

61 Adoration of the Magi. Page from the Queen Mary Psalter. British Museum, London.

picture of agony rather than redemption. Another side of German art appears in the exquisite workmanship of the charming colourful domed reliquary shown here [**60**]—a gilded copper Byzantine church with solemn ivory inhabitants.

In Italy, Roman and Byzantine influences remained strong, and Gothic was rarely used in its pure form for building. Trade links with Byzantium and the Near East encouraged the continued use of mosaics instead of stained glass, and in the Doge's Palace at Venice [**62**] the windows are small and the strongly patterned walls are Eastern in feeling. Instead of the spires and vertical lines found on town halls in the north, the palace is in the ancient flat-roofed Mediterranean tradition.

English illuminators in East Anglia formed a distinct school in the 14th century. In the page shown here [**61**], there is an interesting contrast between the graceful formal *Adoration of the Magi* and the quick and natural sketch at the bottom. The artist was skilful enough to make the main scene more 'lifelike' but thought his patterns and colours more appropriate to an important scene.

This refined decorative quality appears increasingly in in 14th-century Gothic art. One reason was that developing towns and splendid courts demanded a more worldly sophisticated art, culminating in the elongated figures and delicate observation of nature of the 15th-century 'International Gothic' style. One of the masterpieces of the style is the *Très Riches Heures du Duc de Berry* by the Limbourg brothers; in this page, the month of March [**64**], there is a new sensitivity to the life of the countryside, shown by the loving accumulation of detail. For the first time for centuries

secular patronage was leading to secular art—a rich man taking pleasure in his earthly possessions. The Middle Ages were coming to a end.

Decorative elements also began to proliferate in cathedral architecture. The trend was anticipated in England, where by 1280 the 'Early English' Gothic of Salisbury and Lincoln was giving way to the 'Decorated' Gothic style. Tracery, originally bars of stone used as window supports, spread over cathedral interiors in sinuous ribbon-like patterns that are amazing in a material so apparently intractable. Outside, the emphasis on height and vertical effect became still more pronounced, and buildings assumed an attenuated, seemingly fragile appearance. The French 'Flamboyant' ('flame-like') style developed under the influence of English Decorated into a spiky ornateness.

As if in reaction, 15th-century English architecture took on a new simplicity, running counter to the whole European trend. In Perpendicular, as the name suggests, the emphasis is again on clean vertical lines; the walls are like grids to hold glass. Decoration is concentrated on the ceilings, where the verticals radiate into rounded, ribbed, fan-like structures called fan-vaults. The chapel [**63**] at King's College, Cambridge, represents a fitting climax to the style: the disciplined pattern of stonework gives an effect of great splendour, while the almost total absence of walls lends the whole interior an extraordinary lightness and delicacy.

With hindsight, all these developments give the impression that late medieval art had become gracefully effete or overburdened, and that it was ready to give place to something new and more vigorous.

62 Doge's Palace, Venice.

63 King's College chapel, Cambridge.

64 Limbourg brothers: The Month of March. Page from the illuminated manuscript 'Les Très Riches Heures du Duc de Berry'. Musée Condé, Chantilly.

The Renaissance in Italy

As Europe emerged from the Middle Ages, the simple society dominated by church and castle began to give way to a more sophisticated city culture. At the same time there was an astonishing outburst of artistic creativity which is known as the Renaissance. The changes brought by the Renaissance differed from country to country, but the new spirit first showed itself in Italy, and also reached its climax there. Italy was now the wealthiest country in Europe. It was made up of independent city-states such as Florence and Venice, which had grown rich by trading with the East and supplying the rest of Europe with eagerly sought-after luxury goods. In an atmosphere of lavish display, merchant princes and bankers competed with dictators and dukes to commission the leading artists and entice them to their cities and courts.

The sources of Italian art were Byzantine and Gothic—the first a long-established tradition, the second an alien style from northern Europe, never wholly accepted by the Italians. Siena held to these traditions longer than any other Italian city, producing two great painters in Duccio and his pupil Simone Martini. Martini's *Annunciation* [65] is typical of the refined Byzantine style, with its graceful postures, fluttering draperies and richly gilded background; the painting is set in an elegant frame of pointed Gothic arches. If we compare the *Annunciation* with Giotto's *Lamentation* [66], we can see at once that they are in quite different styles. Giotto is generally considered the first great Renaissance painter. He discarded traditional ideas in order to emphasise the dramatic and human significance of the events he was painting. Instead of stereotypes, he portrays each person as an individual, capable of expressing his grief with resignation, passion or despair. Our sense of watching a real three-dimensional event is heightened by the use of full modelled forms and foreshortening, and by the inclusion of a background of real objects (the barren hill and tree).

Giotto's innovations were not immediately followed everywhere in Italy; Simone Martini, for example, continued to work in the Byzantine-Gothic style after Giotto's death in 1336. And for the rest of the century the old traditions continued to flourish alongside the new ideas.

In the 15th century the centre of artistic activity was Florence. It was also a centre at which the philosophy

and literature of ancient Greece and Rome were studied with passionate attention. Admiration of the Ancient World became so intense that men began to look on the recent past as an unfortunate interlude, a 'middle age' between the glorious 'classical' age of Antiquity and the present. They tried to write, think and even live like Romans—a revivalist attitude that led later writers to call the whole period a renaissance or 'rebirth'. This attitude strongly influenced artists, who began to look with fresh eyes at Roman remains they had previously taken for granted. But Antiquity was more than a source of knowledge or models: it was a means of realising new drives towards individual self-expression and the exploration of life and nature. And for artists it was a starting-point from which they moved into new realms of experience, emotion and technique.

The inspiration of the Antique is clearest in sculpture and architecture. The great Florentine sculptor at the beginning of the century was Lorenzo Ghiberti, whose most famous work was a series of bronze reliefs for the doors of the Florentine baptistery. Ghiberti won the commission in competition after submitting a trial relief, *The Sacrifice of Isaac* [67]. This has a Gothic delicacy of detail, but the figure of Isaac is most significant, for it was inspired by a Roman sculpture of a captive Barbarian.

Two of Ghiberti's defeated rivals, Donatello and Brunelleschi, apparently left for Rome immediately after the competition, the first to study Antique sculpture, the second Antique architecture. Donatello was to become the outstanding sculptor of 15th-century Florence. He reproduced the physical forms of Antique sculpture, but also struck a new note by imbuing them with a powerful dramatic force. His equestrian monument to Gattamelata [70], the great Paduan mercenary, was inspired by the Roman statue of Marcus Aurelius which is now in Michelangelo's Capitoline Square, Rome. But in spite of his Roman costume, Gattamelata is not a tame copy but a vigorous interpretation of a contemporary hero.

Meanwhile, Brunelleschi's enthusiasm for the ancient monuments of Rome was proving infectious. The most important of the Florentine architects who followed his example was Alberti, who not only built churches and palaces but also published a treatise on architecture. Soon Roman ground plans and Roman

ornamentation began to appear in Florentine architecture. From that time forward, the triangular pediment, fluted columns and pilasters, the semicircular arch and Doric, Ionic and Corinthian capitals were used throughout Western architecture as a matter of course until the 20th century.

In the 1520s Brunelleschi designed the dome of Florence cathedral [69], a complicated brick construction which still stands as proof of his engineering genius. He also calculated the mathematical laws governing perspective (the technique of giving an illusion of depth on a flat surface). This discovery was to be of immense importance to painters, and one of the first to exploit it was Masaccio. Like Giotto, Masaccio concentrated on the drama of the events he portrayed, avoiding the accumulation of possibly charming but irrelevant detail. The use of perspective allowed him to emphasise the significance of the subject-matter; in the *Tribute Money* [68], for example, the simple gestures and the placing of the figures as if in depth draw our attention to the central figure of Christ.

Masaccio's austere style influenced painters like Fra Angelico and Fra Filippo Lippi, but it scarcely reflected popular taste. The wealthy merchants who ruled Florence were generous patrons, but they could not resist the glitter of gold and the desire for self-glorification. They preferred painters like Uccello, whose real gift was for decoration. (He seems to have been fascinated by perspective, but never got it quite right.) His *Rout of San Romano* [71] is not at all life-like or dramatic, but a charming, curiously formal version of a popular local victory against Siena.

The *Rout* was painted for a member of the Medici family, who appear again in Botticelli's *Adoration of the Magi* [73]. Here they are seen in all their finery, worshipping at the Nativity; notice the elegant Roman ruins in the background. Botticelli had a very personal lyrical style which married solid forms with a strong sense of line and pattern. Two of his most famous works, *The Birth of Venus* and the *Primavera*, are based on Greco-Roman mythology, which was for centuries to be one of the chief subjects of painting and sculpture.

The linear quality of Botticelli's paintings may have had something to do with his training as a goldsmith. Artists often trained in one craft and ended by practising several; painters like Pollaiuolo and Verrocchio,

66 Giotto: The Lamentation over the Dead Body of Christ. Fresco in the Arena chapel, Padua.

67 Ghiberti: The Sacrifice of Isaac. Bronze relief. Museo Nazionale, Florence.

68 Masaccio: The Tribute Money. Church of the Carmine, Florence.

69

70

71

69 Brunelleschi: Dome of Florence cathedral.

70 Donatello: Gattamelata. Padua.

71 Uccello: The Rout of San Romano. Uffizi, Florence.

72 Piero della Francesca: The Resurrection. Fresco in the Palazzo Communale, Borgo San Sepolcro.

73 Botticelli: Adoration of the Magi. Uffizi, Florence.

for example, were also sculptors and goldsmiths. The general Renaissance ideal of the 'universal man' had its equivalent here in the omnicompetent Florentine artist. Painting was approached as a craft like any other, to be learned through an apprenticeship in a painter's workshop.

The serious monumental style of Giotto and Masaccio culminates in the paintings of Piero della Francesca. Piero was not a Florentine but worked mainly in Umbria, just to the south. He was fascinated by Antique forms and by theories of proportion. His compositions are calculated with mathematical precision, and his feeling for abstract shapes gives them a fine balance and serenity. *The Resurrection* [72] is pervaded by a great silence, as if time has been suspended, making all the more moving the triumph of life over death. Although unrecognised until recently, Piero is now widely considered one of the finest of all 15th-century Italian painters.

In northern Italy the greatest 15th-century painter was probably Mantegna, who lived and worked at Mantua for the Gonzaga family. He was a scholar and archaeologist as well as a painter, and set himself to give a historically accurate account of Roman life. *The Triumph of Caesar* [74] gave him a wonderful excuse for a lively scene in which he could show off his knowledge of clothing, vases, urns and other trappings of Antiquity. Perhaps more than any other painter, Mantegna epitomises the 15th-century nostalgia for the glory that was Rome. He was, incidentally, the son-in-law of Jacopo Bellini, whose sons Gentile and Giovanni were leaders of the Venetian Renaissance.

Art and artists were now beginning to hold a very different place in society. Competitive patronage and Renaissance individualism gave artists a new sense of worth. The last vestige of their medieval anonymity disappeared, and in the next century the artist emerged as a unique and sometimes eccentric individual or 'genius', so esteemed that, like any emperor or king, he found enthusiastic biographers. Works of art were no longer always part of a decorative scheme or linked with worship; the easel-painting, for example, is essentially an object intended to be looked at for its own sake – a wholly modern revolutionary change.

During the 16th century – the 'High Renaissance' – Florence continued to produce great artists; but its position as the centre of Italian art was taken over by Rome, where ambitious Popes like Leo X and Julius II were bent on glorifying the city and themselves. The High Renaissance is personified by three of the greatest artists of all time: the Florentines Leonardo da Vinci and Michelangelo, and Raphael Sanzio from Urbino.

The Renaissance ideal of the universal man was realised in Leonardo (1452–1519). In him, scientific curiosity and powerful intelligence were allied with love of nature and a deep feeling for the mysteries of the universe. By his own account engineer, scientist, musician, painter and sculptor, Leonardo studied everything, from the movement of water to the internal complexities of the human body; he made designs for flying machines, dams, buildings, siege machines, all sketched and described in mirror-writing in his notebooks. He painted what has become the most famous picture in the world – the *Mona Lisa*, the woman who sits, smiling mysteriously, before a melting landscape of rocks and water. In *The Virgin of the Rocks* [77], the

74 Mantegna: The Triumph of Caesar (detail). Royal Collection, Hampton Court Palace.

75 Michelangelo: David. Accademia, Florence.

76 Michelangelo: The Creation of Man. Fresco on the Sistine chapel ceiling, Vatican.

rocks appear to be lit by the figures themselves, who give out a radiance that seems to come from within them. The gentle modelling of the faces, with their sweet half-smiles, and the play of unearthly light—typical of Leonardo—exercised an immediate and powerful fascination on contemporary painters. Leonardo's experiments with painting materials in *The Last Supper* led to its partial disintegration within his lifetime, and he often left works half-finished; it was as if his genius was flawed, standing in the way of completion or completeness. Of all his projects, only a few paintings now survive.

Raphael (1483–1520) is the master of harmony. In his youth, already a prodigy, he went to Florence, where he was influenced by both Leonardo and Michelangelo. While Michelangelo was working on the Sistine ceiling, Raphael was painting the frescoes of the Stanze, a suite of rooms in the Vatican. Two of these, the *School of Athens* and the *Disputà*, are famous masterpieces of the High Renaissance. Beautifully composed, clear and calm, they radiate serenity. Raphael was an outstanding portrait painter, and he also developed the type of Madonna, pure and idealised, that was to be the model for generations of painters. *The Marriage of the Virgin* [78] shows him in lyrical mood; the temple in the background, a complicated exercise in perspective, looks forward to Raphael's later work as an architect.

Michelangelo (1475–1564) was born before Raphael and outlived him by forty years, and his genius and vast undertakings in all the arts made him the idol of generations of artists. Michelangelo's art is dramatic, intense and violent. Obsessed with the human body, he created a monumental image of man as Herculean and heroic, the central figure in the drama of God's universe. The frescoes [76] on the ceiling of the Sistine

77 Leonardo da Vinci: The Virgin of the Rocks. National Gallery, London.

78 Raphael: The Marriage of the Virgin. Brera, Milan.

78

chapel in Rome give the fullest expression to this vision, a panorama of Biblical history from the Creation onwards. Thirty years later Michelangelo painted the *Last Judgment* over the altar of the chapel—a violent feverish work foreshadowing the Mannerists and filled with mighty forms writhing under sentence of damnation.

Michelangelo thought of himself as a sculptor rather than a painter, and in fact his painted images of man have the solidity of sculpted forms. His early *David* [75] is at first sight 'Greek' in spite of its colossal size (nearly seventeen feet high). But unlike the sculptures of Antiquity, Michelangelo's heroes are men who have known trouble and doubt, noble but not serene. In his mature sculptures their turmoil is even more apparent, invading the very muscles and sinews.

Michelangelo was also an architect. He built the first modern square on the Capitoline Hill in Rome, and completed the finest Renaissance palace, the Farnese. In 1547 he took over the rebuilding of St Peter's in Rome, which had been planned and partly rebuilt by others. The chief feature he added was the dome, actually erected to his design some twenty years after his death; the emphatic solids and voids created by its ribs and columns show once again how sculptural his thinking was.

Donato Bramante had made the first designs for the new St Peter's. Heavily influenced by Roman architecture in scale, structure and ornament, his buildings are simple, solid and almost austere. The Venetian Andrea Palladio was still closer in spirit to the old Roman world. Palladio gave his name to a whole style of building for aristocratic country houses, based on Roman villas. His Villa Rotonda [79] at Vicenza is a fine example of 'Palladian' strength and simplicity; the perfect symmetry and the use of a temple portico are typical features.

In contrast to the 'intellectual' painting of Florence and Rome, Venice produced an art in which colours rather than lines and shapes strike the eye. Titian was a painter universally admired in his own very long lifetime (1487?–1576). He was particularly renowned as a portraitist: his painting of the Holy Roman Emperor Charles V on horseback was the model for later European portraits of royalty, and his *Charles V Seated* [80] is a superbly composed, compassionate study of the weary ruler of half the world. As Titian grew older, his style evolved into a kind of impressionism in which shades of colour created or suggested shapes, replacing lines; a hint of this can be seen in the landscape behind Charles.

Titian was influenced in his early years by Giorgione, a brilliant exponent of the landscape, which was a Venetian speciality. *The Tempest* [81] is a work full of mystery and an indefinable feeling of suspense; the landscape surrounding the two strange figures is bathed with the brilliant ominous light associated with approaching storms, throwing trees and buildings into

79

80

79 Palladio:
Villa Rotonda,
Vicenza.

80 Titian:
Charles V
Seated.
Pinakothek,
Munich.

81 Giorgione: The Tempest. Accademia di Belle Arti, Venice.

relief and casting deep shadows.

Other great Venetian artists were the brilliant decorator Veronese; Correggio, supreme painter of voluptuous nudes; and Tintoretto, whose vast dramatic canvases are crammed with figures in violent movement. Tintoretto's work is close to Mannerism, a development of the Renaissance style that began in central Italy. After about 1530 it looked as though art had reached perfection with Michelangelo, Leonardo and Raphael; further progress seemed impossible. The Mannerists attempted to escape from this dead-end by exaggerating, dramatising and distorting elements in High Renaissance art, as Michelangelo did in his late works like the *Last Judgment*. Their colours tended to be harsh and unnatural, and their drawing over-refined; in their compositions they strained after violent and novel effects for their own sake. Parmigianino, an early Mannerist, often created sinuous elongated figures, full of ecstasy. *Cupid Carving His Bow* [83] is more robust but equally Mannerist in its arch eroticism—and look at Cupid's tricky, unnatural posture, and the coy little boys framed by his legs! Bronzino was the greatest exponent of the Mannerist portrait; his sitters are clear-eyed and unmoved, rendered with cold skill. Benvenuto Cellini had a great reputation in his lifetime for gold and silver works of amazing technical skill—most of them unfortunately lost; today he is remembered for his racy and self-congratulatory *Autobiography*, his bronze *Perseus*, and a sumptuous and elegant saltcellar [82] made about 1540 for Francis I of France.

By this time Italian artists and craftsmen were being employed in many parts of Europe, and Italian styles were being grafted more or less happily on to native traditions. But these traditions were no longer everywhere late Gothic: some areas of northern Europe had already had their own kind of 'Renaissance'.

82 The Royal Salt, made of gold, enamel and precious stones by Benvenuto Cellini. Kunsthistorisches Museum, Vienna.

83 Parmigianino: Cupid Carving His Bow. Kunsthistorisches Museum, Vienna.

The Northern Renaissance

Outside Italy, Gothic remained the accepted building style even in the 15th century, and the International Gothic style of painting was practised by such great masters as the Limbourgs (see page 48). But new forces were already at work. From about 1380 the Flemish sculptor Claus Sluter worked for the Duke of Burgundy, just as the Limbourgs did, but his sculptures have a dramatic realism that contrasts strongly with the world of the miniatures. Sluter's *Madonna and Child* [84] is a forthright expressive work in which the drapery is no longer smoothly elegant but swirls vigorously, leading the eye from the figure of Mary to the Child on her arm. The figures are not static but caught in movement; however the moment is also one of intense communion between Mother and Child. Sluter's break with the medieval tradition is the northern equivalent of Donatello's reaction against the over-refinement of the International Gothic style.

The influence of Sluter's work was especially strong in Germany, where the new feeling of life and vigour was captured by artists like Veit Stoss, whose sculptures (especially wood-carvings) combine greater realism with emotional force.

The most radical developments in 15th-century painting occurred in the Low Countries ('Flanders'). There, as in Italy, wealthy cities and a prosperous merchant class favoured a more realistic art. The most important northern painter of the century, Jan van Eyck, was a Fleming and, like so many others, did a good deal of work for the dukes of Burgundy. His vast Ghent altarpiece is still largely medieval in feeling, but *The Madonna with the Chancellor Rolin* [85], painted in about 1435, is full of sharp realistic detail. In fact it was through accumulation of details (as in a miniature) that northern painters approached realism — unlike, for example, the Italians Giotto and Masaccio. Here peacocks strut on the terrace and little birds hop about in the flowerbeds; you can almost feel the texture of Rolin's heavy brocaded coat, the faceted jewels set in the hem of the Virgin's cloak, the cold smoothness of the marble floor. Even the materials the painter used were different: van Eyck perfected the use of oil colours, which, unlike the tempera and fresco of the Italians, lends itself to building up detail and achieving a glossy textured surface. On the other hand the style of the arcaded terrace and van Eyck's use of perspective to give his picture depth show his knowledge of Italian

84

art—and, incidentally, the impression made by Italian fashions on northern patrons.

Northern feeling for detail does not lead to a showy empty display of technical skill. There is a deep seriousness in van Eyck's work, and his great contemporary Rogier van der Weyden often achieves an almost unbearable intensity of religious emotion. Flemish painting was much admired in Italy, and Hugo van der Goes' altarpiece [86], painted for the Italian businessman Tommaso Portinari, caused a sensation when it was first seen in Florence. The deeply religious tone, the tenderness of the rough shepherds, the sumptuous details, all had a profound influence on Florentine painters.

In the course of the 15th century the fashion for things Italian carried everything before it. Flemish painters like Mabuse went to Italy as artistic pilgrims,

and came back captivated by Italian styles and new subjects such as mythology and the nude. But the native tradition was never completely submerged, and in Hieronymus Bosch and Peter Brueghel the Elder, Flanders produced two great painters who were wholly unitalianate.

The strange genius of Hieronymus Bosch seems to have been untouched by the Renaissance spirit. His amazing, inventively grotesque imagery has led the Surrealists and other painters of fantasy and nightmare to claim him as an ancestor; but the feeling in his paintings is closer to the puritanical world-hating side of the Middle Ages. The pain and sorrow of life, the bad after-taste of pleasure, temptations that are lurid and disgusting, Hell at the end of it all—these are presented literally and symbolically in *The Garden of Earthly Delights* [87].

85

84 Sluter: Madonna and Child. Chartreuse de Champmol, Dijon.

85 Jan van Eyck: The Madonna with the Chancellor Rolin. Louvre, Paris.

87

86 Hugo van der Goes: Adoration of the Shepherds. Central panel of the Portinari altarpiece. Uffizi, Florence.

87 Bosch: Hell. Inside of the right-hand panel of the 'Garden of Earthly Delights' triptych. Prado, Madrid.

88 Dürer: Adam and Eve. Engraving. British Museum, London.

89 Breughel: Peasant Dance. Kunsthistorisches Museum, Vienna.

90 Cranach: Venus and Cupid. Borghese Gallery, Rome.

88

89

Common people and common pursuits are right at the centre of Brueghel's art, painted for their own sake and with immense zest. He made no attempt to idealise the heavy graceless figures brawling, boozing and clumping about in the *Peasant Dance* [89]. In many of his pictures it seems the other way round; his people seem so bloated or brutal or slyly lustful that we find them rather repulsive without being able to feel sure whether the painter's obvious pleasure in the scene carries with it any element of satire. Brueghel did show the blacker side of life—beggars, cripples, outcasts—and his *Massacre of the Innocents* translated the Bible into a dreadful contemporary event, reminiscent of the horrors of 16th-century religious wars and peasant revolts.

By the 16th century the new invention of printing from movable type was making manuscript books obsolete—and with them the art of the miniaturist. It was replaced by techniques that made it possible to reproduce many copies of the same picture. The first of these techniques was the woodcut, which involves cutting away areas of a block of wood, leaving a raised relief which is inked and printed on to paper. The woodcut made bold striking prints, but was superseded by the engraving, which gave far more subtle and detailed effects. Engraving reverses the woodcut process: lines cut into wood or metal form channels that will hold ink; the surface of the block is wiped clean and the ink left in the channels prints on to the paper.

Engraving became a great European art, and also a source of information. Thanks to the relative cheapness and quantity of printed books, artists anywhere could now find out quickly through engravings what was being done in other countries. Though the medium had its own specialists, the first great engraver was the German painter Albrecht Dürer. In many ways Dürer was a man of the Renaissance. After his apprenticeship in Nuremberg he had studied in Italy; and like the great Italian masters he was recognised as a genius in his own lifetime. Like Leonardo he tried to reach the heart of the mysteries of life and beauty; his drawings—such as the famous hare and the clump of grass—show his unquenchable curiosity and sense of wonder. But his paintings, though often 'Italian', include many self-portraits that show a typically northern inward-looking spirit. And in engravings such as *The Four Horsemen of the Apocalypse* a vision of life as senseless and full of horror is stated with an emotional extremism hardly ever found in Mediterranean art. *Adam and Eve* [88] shows both sides of Dürer. The poses, proportions and drawing of the figures are Italian, the background of trees and handling of detail northern—for example the mouse and sleepy domestic cat whose peaceful life together is about to be ended by the eating of the fateful apple.

The German ideal of female beauty can be seen in the

pert, small-breasted, full-bellied nudes of Dürer's contemporary Lukas Cranach [90]; these charming little creatures have little in common with the Venus-figures of Antiquity [23] which are their originals. The revolutionary art of Albrecht Altdorfer brought out another facet of the northern genius: in his paintings, landscape is shown purely for its own sake, with verdant massy trees and foliage, and overwhelming skies. To the powerful traditions of German religious art, expressed for example in distorted tormented wood-carvings [59], the painter Grünewald [92] brought an unequalled colour sense, and the intensity of his own brand of realism gives added power to the northern preoccupation with the sufferings of this world.

The Protestant Reformation in the early 16th century had important repercussions on painting. Where Protestantism took hold, there was far less demand for the kind of religious art that was used to decorate Catholic churches. Secular patronage – and secular subjects – became increasingly important. Germany was torn by religious wars, and the career of one German painter, Hans Holbein, was so affected that he moved to England, where he became Henry VIII's court painter. Portraits such as *Jane Seymour* [91] are typical of his calm, beautifully observed art. Native English art remained largely uninspired, although charming delicate miniatures were painted for lockets and brooches by Nicholas Hilliard and Isaac Oliver.

France was more susceptible to the Renaissance than her neighbours, and by the 16th century Italian influence was very strong. Leonardo worked for Francis I just before his death, and Francis imported leading Mannerist artists like Cellini, Primaticcio and Rosso to create a distinctive kind of decoration at Fontainebleau. Native French art is typified by the cool graceful sculptures of Jean Goujon, and the penetrating portraits of Jean Clouet.

A grand religious art was produced in Catholic Spain by El Greco ('the Greek'), who was by birth a Cretan. El Greco studied in Venice before moving to Toledo in about 1570, and his style owes something to the theatricality and violence of Tintoretto and the Mannerists. But in the devout formal atmosphere of imperial Spain he developed a highly idiosyncratic, hallucinatory style like nothing before it, with strange intense colours, metallic highlights, elongated sinuous forms and stiff frozen draperies and clouds. In *The Burial of Count Orgaz* [93] heaven and earth are in contact for a moment (one of the mourners seems to have noticed the fact), and the wild splendour of the one makes a fascinating contrast with the sombre pomp of the other. For us it is a fitting evocation of 16th-century Spain, the dominant power in Europe and conqueror of the newly found Americas.

91

92

91 Holbein: Jane Seymour. Kunsthistorisches Museum,
Vienna.

92 Grünewald: Crucifixion. Samuel H. Kress Collection,
National Gallery of Art, Washington.

93 El Greco: The Burial of Count Orgaz. Santo Tomé, Toledo.

93

The Americas before Columbus

Within fifty years of discovering America, Europeans had destroyed the two great 'Pre-Columbian' empires: the empire of the Aztecs in Central America (Mexico), and of the Incas on the east coast of South America (Peru). Both were high cultures with great cities, civic and religious systems, and developed arts and crafts. Though we tend to talk loosely of the Aztec and Inca civilisations, the names are merely those of the dominant people in each area when the Spaniards arrived. Their history of these areas stretches back over three thousand years, and their cultures were developed and diversified by several peoples; in Central America, for example, Olmecs, Mayas, Toltecs, Mixtecs and others had come and gone before the Aztec conquests of the 14th century, building and finally abandoning great cities like Chichén Itzá, which lay overgrown and forgotten until rediscovered by explorers and archaeologists.

The same thing happened to the religious centre at Teotihuacán, which was thronged by worshippers at a period roughly contemporary with the European Dark Ages. One of its great monuments is the Pyramid of the Sun [94], a restrained and simplified version of the stepped pyramid also found (as the ziggurat) in early Mesopotamian cultures. Inca buildings were made of uncemented blocks of stone, like Stonehenge [5] and Mycenean architecture.

Sculpture was practised in several styles, from the naturalistic to the grotesque; the best-known are probably continuous undulating relief patterns of monstrous human and animal forms, produced by the Aztecs. Work in gold and semi-precious stones was magnificent. A distinctive feature was the use of turquoise mosaic; here the brilliant coloured stone brings to life a two headed snake [96], a rhythmic vibrant Central American version of a creature found in creation myths of many cultures.

Textiles and pottery were made in America outside as well as inside Mexico and Peru. Here, as in primitive cultures in other parts of the world, highly sophisticated weaving techniques were developed. The Mochica pottery of Peru, produced several hundred years before the Incas founded their empire, is the most interesting. It was made in two halves in a mould, fitted with a combined double spout and handle, and painted and polished. Often it was given a modelled head (human, animal or mythical), as on this piece [95]. These human-headed pots, which occur in widely separated areas all round the Pacific, are thought to be connected with the veneration of ancestor skulls and consequently with head-hunting. This one, from a sophisticated and mature South American culture, was certainly intended as a less gruesome substitute for a captured trophy.

There were many less advanced cultures, including the North American 'Red Indian' peoples: the Pueblo of the south-west, who built often enormous structures of stone and adobe (dried mud); the 'mound-builders' of the Ohio-Mississippi region, whose high burial mounds were furnished with realistically carved pipes and other goods; and the north-west coast Indians. These last were scattered in fishing communities along the seaboard of Oregon, Canada and southern Alaska. They had abundant timber, with which they carved and painted figures, masks, houses and utensils in a very forceful accurate style. Easily their most famous works, however, are totem poles, set up during life and after death to tell all and sundry which totem (animal) group the owner belonged to, and to display other marks of his rank or status. Hidden in the part of the continent furthest from Europeans, the north-west coast culture remained intact down to recent times, making it possible for us to enjoy an art created from materials that might all too easily have perished or been destroyed.

94 The Pyramid of the Sun, Mexico.

95 Pottery vessel from Peru in the shape of a human head. Museum für Völkerkunde, Munich.

96 Turquoise ornament from Mexico. British Museum, London.

95

96

Later Eastern Art

Civilisations generally remain great while they are nourished by influences from outside. The truth of this can be seen in the arts of the East: Indian art was revitalised by contact with Islam, whereas China's withdrawal into isolation stifled creativity, despite all the skills and technical knowledge of her artists and craftsmen.

Arab invaders appeared in India as early as the 8th century, and in the Middle Ages much of northern India was controlled by Muslim dynasties. In the 16th century the Mughals, a ruling line of Mongol origin, established a great empire with twin capitals at Agra and Delhi. The empire was at its height under Akbar (1556–1605) and his successors Jahangir and Shah Jahan, in whose reigns a distinctive Indo-Muslim art was created.

In the magnificent palaces and mosques of the Mughal period, the many terraces and the general sense of profusion derive from Hindu architecture, while the domes and clean lines are Islamic. Tomb monuments are a distinguished feature of Mughal art – palatial, multi-domed mausolea laid out on platforms and richly decorated. It comes as a shock to realise that the splendid Taj Mahal [98], one of the most famous buildings in the world, is not a pleasure dome but just a mausoleum, built at Agra by Shah Jahan for his dearly loved wife Mahal. The dazzling exterior is white marble, sumptuously decorated with relief carving and inlaid coloured stones. Here there is little to remind us of Hindu art, and a glance back at Ajanta [30] and Angkor Wat [31] reveals the difference between the organic sculpturesque quality of Hindu building and Islamic abstraction and purity of line.

The other great Mughal art, miniature painting for book illustration, was even more distinctively Muslim. The Persian miniature was the original model for Mughal artists, and famous Persian painters were brought to work at the Indian courts. But even when their subject is everyday life Persian paintings have a rather remote air, with decorative rather than realistic colours. Mughal artists are much more successful in conveying a sense of involvement and strenuous activity. The bustle and surprise of the night attack comes over at once in this page [97] from a book made for Akbar (the *Hamza-nahmeh*, the first great achievement of the independent Mughal style); compare it with the patterned miniature from Persia [50].

The Chinese looked more and more to the great days of the past. When the Yuan Mongols were expelled by the native Ming dynasty (1368–1644), statesmen and artists made a determined attempt to restore the old rather than strive to create new forms and ideas; and the Ch'ing or Manchu dynasty (1644–1912), despite its 'barbarian' origins, refused all meaningful contact with the outside world until traumatically confronted with the Western gunboat.

One aspect of this backward-looking spirit was rigid state control of the arts, especially by the early Ming emperors. The Ming built massive temple halls for their ancestors, and also splendid tombs, the routes to which are lined with large stone figures of men and beasts. Like the lion seen here [100] they are impressive despite a certain crudity, and seem to have been consciously designed in imitation of T'ang sculptures of six hundred years before.

The finest products of the later dynasties were porcelain and lacquer. Porcelain from the imperial factories at Ching-te-chen reached an unsurpassed technical brilliance with such famous types as the green-glazed celadon wares and 'blue-and-white', in which decorations were painted in cobalt blue under a transparent glaze. Under the Ch'ing many porcelain vessels were exquisitely decorated with enamel colours painted over the glaze. These pieces are usually classified into rose, green or black 'families' according to the predominant colour in the design; the delicate little

birds and flowers on this 'famille rose' bottle [99] capture the civilised man's dream of nature as a world of harmony and delight.

Porcelain—hard, thin, translucent, brilliantly white— fascinated Europeans more than any other Chinese product; and the more so since for centuries they tried unsuccessfully to discover and imitate the Chinese techniques. The establishment of European traders at Macao and Canton led to the export of quantities of porcelain, silks and lacquer to the West, often decorated with 'Chinese' designs invented solely to match up to the European idea of 'Oriental' taste. In the long run, overproduction and vulgarisation led to a decline in

97 A Night Attack. Painting from the 'Hamza-Nameh'. Rogers Fund 1918, Metropolitan Museum of Art, New York.

98 The Taj Mahal at Agra.

99 'Famille rose' porcelain bottle. Ch'ing dynasty. Percival David Foundation of Chinese Art, London.

100 Lion on the Sacred Way leading to the tomb of the Emperor Yung-Lo at Nan-K'ou. Ming dynasty.

101 The Phoenix Hall at Uji, near Kyoto.

9⟨

1⟨

standards; and the disorders of the 19th century gave the death-blow to this last of the great arts of China.

Japan was much more isolated than China, and deeply dependent on her. For centuries this was a matter of geography: China was the only accessible source of civilised custom, style and knowledge, and the history of Japanese culture is largely a pattern of absorption of Chinese influence and reaction against it. Later, isolation became a deliberate choice; after brief contact with the West the Japanese expelled traders and missionaries alike, stamped out Christianity and successfully ignored the very existence of the outside world. Only in 1854 did the West, in the person of the American Commodore Perry, break in upon Japanese seclusion.

The recorded history of Japan begins in the 6th century AD, under the stimulus of 'imports' from China: Buddhism, ideas of imperial government, a script that was adapted to the Japanese language, and art objects. Buddhism produced a strong tradition of sculpture, and even prompted occasional Japanese excursions into monumentality such as the 42-foot bronze Buddha at Kamakura. Chinese models were followed in the arts down to about the 11th century, when distinctive native elements began to appear. For example, the curved roofs of the Phoenix Hall [101]

near Kyoto are typical of Far Eastern architecture, but the posts raising the building above the ground are specifically Japanese, accentuating the impression of exquisite fragility; the setting, and in particular the calm proximity of water, greatly enhances the effect.

During this period Kyoto was the centre of a sophisticated, somewhat decadent court life in which, as in 18th-century France, women gave the tone to society and created such masterpieces of literature as Lady Murasaki's *Tales of Genji*. The illustration of books and poems became a Japanese speciality, and one to which their gift for vivid and economical use of line was particularly well adapted.

Temperamental bias towards bold and effective use of line was reinforced by the introduction of monochrome (single-colour) ink painting, which was brought from China by Zen Buddhist monks. One of the most interesting of many Zen contributions to Japanese art was the 'priest portrait'. This was a sort of icon carrying a portrait of a spiritual teacher; it was presented to a successful student, who was supposed to meditate before it. The example shown here [103], an ink painting of the monk Ikkyu, is exceptional in its realism and force.

Painting proper—that is, in more than one colour—developed through the agency of decorative artists

101

working on doors and folding screens. They applied their colours in large flat areas, often in combination with a uniform background of gold leaf—a technique that harmonises perfectly with a linear style. This art reached a climax of subtlety and naturalness in the work of the 18th-century painter Ogata Korin.

Flat strong colours and incisive outlines characterise the more popular art of the colour woodcut. Prints taken from wood blocks could be produced cheaply and quickly in large numbers, and were designed to appeal to middle class townspeople interested in sex, sentiment, the theatre and incidents of ordinary life. The first master of the colour print was Suzuki Harunobu (1725–70), famous for charming studies of women and children in everyday domestic settings. The lady with the cat [102], though a character from the *Tales of Genji*, is posed prosaically in an ordinary interior, and might represent any citizen's wished-for lover. Such a 'vulgar' available art had only a modest reputation among cultivated Japanese. But when it reached the West—sometimes in the form of wrapping-paper—it deeply influenced revolutionary artists like Manet, Toulouse-Lautrec and Whistler; and to this day the 19th-century masters Hokusai, Hiroshige and Utamaro remain for most Westerners the supreme Japanese artists.

102 Haronobu: Woman and her Young Sister with a Cat. Colour woodcut.

103 Bokusai: Ikkyu Sojan. National Museum, Tokyo.

Baroque, Rococo and Realism

The Italian Mannerists had had their day, but Italian creativity was far from being exhausted. 17th-century Rome was the birthplace of a style filled with the assured triumphant spirit of the Counter-Reformation —as Mannerism had perhaps mirrored the uncertainties of shaken faith. This Baroque style, though adapted to villas and palaces, was essentially Catholic and devotional, expressing a mood new to religious art.

The life-size marble figures of Gianlorenzo Bernini's *Ecstasy of St Teresa* [**105**] shows us what that mood was. The saint lies in a swoon as the angel of the Lord prepares to pierce her with the arrow of divine love. Here faith is not serene, but a violent emotion that racks the physical frame as well as the spirit—an effect conveyed by St Teresa's expression and posture, the disordered mass of her habit, and the rugged rock-like cloud on which she is being carried to heaven.

Violent emotion gives rise to drama; and the dramatic visual effects of Baroque are largely obtained by manipulating light and space. *St Teresa* is lit from a concealed source above the figures; the light is filtered through yellow glass to simulate sunshine. The setting—a recess surrounded by architectural elements—creates a feeling of depth, so that the whole group seems to float in space, framed like a painting by the columns.

Bernini's sculpture, incidentally, is intended to be looked at from one viewpoint only, unlike Michelangelo's (or Henry Moore's) for instance, which is designed to provide the viewer with many differing aspects as he walks round it.

Sweeping, restlessly moving lines, drama, illusion, a combination of effects drawn from several arts go to make up an art that overwhelms and convinces the spectator. The Baroque church interior is a sacred drama—a total work of art into which individual works and decorations are merged. In its full-blown form the style dates from just such a work: Bernini's decoration and furnishing of St Peter's, which he filled with marble facings, stucco, gilt and statuary, and for which he created the Baldacchino, a bronze canopy with twisted columns, placed over the tomb of St Peter.

Bernini also designed the curving colonnade in front of St Peter's, which enhances so superbly the monumental proportions of this great church. In fact, few men have left their mark so strongly on one city as Bernini has on Rome. A stormy but deeply pious man, he was commissioned many times by the Pope to undertake architectural work of various kinds—tombs, fountains, churches, etc.

In contrast to the solid geometry of Renaissance architecture, Baroque is full of restless lines that seem to swarm around the space they define making the space itself seem like a tangible thing. The masterpiece of another great Roman architect, Francesco Borromini, is San Carlo alle Quattro Fontane [**104**], a little church with interior walls that undulate in a series of curved recesses. A similar effect is achieved on the façade, where there are five recesses around the entrance, given emphasis by the projecting columns and first-storey 'temple'. Instead of the clear-cut triangular pediment at the top of a Renaissance building, there is a balustrade curving up to a decorative oval.

The Baroque spread from Italy into the Catholic lands of Spain, Austria, south Germany and Flanders. The Spaniards took it to Central and South America, where it flourished for centuries. But it met with only limited acceptance in Catholic France and Protestant England and Holland, the three powers to whom the immediate future belonged. In political terms, therefore, this most dynamic of styles was an art of declining states—a situation that it is fascinating, if dangerous, to attempt to explain.

In Spain particularly architects took up the Baroque style with enthusiasm. Indeed, their fervour often overflowed into excess. In Spain, Narciso Tomé's

104 Borromini: San Carlo alle Quattro Fontane, Rome.

106

105 Bernini: The Ecstasy of St Teresa. Cornaro chapel, Santa Maria della Vittoria, Rome.

106 Caravaggio: The Supper at Emmaus. National Gallery, London.

Trasparente altar in Toledo cathedral is an amazing example of ambitious Baroque ornament, a massive tableau of marble and bronze figures apparently suspended miraculously in mid air and lit by a mysterious heavenly light. When it was first completed it was called the eighth wonder of the world. But even the *Trasparente* looks restrained by comparison with the work of José de Churriguera. The excessive over-decoration of his buildings has given rise to the style called 'Churrigueresque'.

In Germany, particularly in the south, the style was also taken up, but with a more controlled enthusiasm in which the details were not allowed to run away with the overall effect. The result was a more completely integrated architectural and decorative style which Balthasar Neumann developed with restrained good taste and dignity into a freshly attractive Rococo, as in his pilgrimage church of Vierzehnheiligen. The style was brought to a triumphant climax by Dominikus Zimmermann in his church of Die Wies, begun in 1745.

In England and France artists and architects tended to prefer more sober styles, mainly taken over from the Renaissance. Resistance to the Baroque was partly a matter of temperament. In France, in particular, there have always been many artists who preferred restrained emotion and clearly defined forms to vividness of colour and expression.

A comparison between the paintings of Caravaggio and Poussin illustrates this difference in temperament.

Michelangelo da Caravaggio was a tempestuous and quarrelsome Italian who was forced to run away from Rome after stabbing his opponent in a tennis match. Caravaggio was the first great Baroque painter, revelling in dramatic contrasts of light and shadow. He was also a realist in his way, painting directly from models who were often poor, old and ugly. But the realism is in the interests of intensity and surprise, as in *The Supper at Emmaus* [106], where Christ sits at a table with worn and ragged peasants, his hands thrust out of the picture towards the viewer.

Nicolas Poussin, the greatest French painter of the 17th century, spent most of his life in Rome but quickly shook off Baroque influence. The qualities of *The Arcadian Shepherds* [107] are harder to appreciate at once than those of Caravaggio's painting, but its restraint, dignity and order have a deep and persistent appeal. Here the drawing is more important than the quiet colouring, and the shepherds and shepherdesses express no great emotion as one of them deciphers the inscription on the tomb, '*et in Arcadia ego*', 'I too am in Arcady' – a reminder that death is present even in the fabled land of rural innocence.

French architects were more directly inspired by

what they knew of the Renaissance, creating solid, rather sober buildings. The growing wealth and power of France was reflected in great country houses (châteaux) and town residences (hôtels), and in the beginnings of town-planning. Under the 'Sun King', Louis XIV, France dominated Europe. The king's château of Versailles was enlarged into a vast palace dedicated to his glory, and was copied by all the aspiring kings and princelings of Europe. Several architects worked on it, notably Louis Le Vau, but Jules Hardouin Mansart, the architect of the Invalides, saw it through to its finished form. Its huge size, superb decorations and formal park setting by André Le Nôtre make Versailles a kingly secular equivalent to the Baroque church.

In England the true Renaissance style was introduced in the early 17th century by a student of the Italian architect Andrea Palladio's writings and works, Inigo Jones, who built the Queen's House at Greenwich and the Banqueting Hall at Whitehall. Later in the century the desire for grandeur of effect led to the use of Baroque elements. St Paul's cathedral [109], built by Sir Christopher Wren after the destruction of the old

cathedral in the Great Fire of London (1666), has a magnificent Renaissance dome, but the coupled columns on the façade, together with the two towers, make the same kind of play with recessed space as Borromini's San Carlo [104]. Two architects who worked with Wren, Nicholas Hawksmoor and Sir John Vanbrugh, built in a Baroque style, though one that was still extremely restrained. Vanbrugh was the architect of Blenheim, the huge palace built at Woodstock for the first Duke of Marlborough. Early in the 18th century a quieter taste reappeared in the cool Palladian style of country houses built by Lord Burlington and his followers, a style directly derived from the great Venetian architect [79].

In the Low Countries there were now two different states: Flanders, a Catholic province of the Spanish empire; and Holland, once the northern portion of Flanders, which had rebelled against Spanish rule and established an independent Protestant republic. Holland was a wealthy sea-power, and her sober merchant class had no use for most forms of Catholic Baroque art—for great domed churches, elaborate altars, vast painted walls and ceilings, or massive sculptures. They were

107

108

men of plain ethical piety and practical interests, using unpretentious houses, churches and civic buildings. The art they were prepared to pay for—and therefore the art they got—consisted above all of easel paintings mirroring the ordinary and visible world. This is a particularly clear case of patronage determining the character of art, and it also proves that art is not necessarily the worse for the restrictions imposed by patrons.

The Dutch demand for paintings was apparently inexhaustible; so much so that painters tended to specialise—in *genre* (scenes of everyday life), still-life (arrangements of objects on their own, without people, animals or landscape), church interiors, marine paintings and landscapes. Portraits were even more popular: portraits of individuals and – a Dutch speciality – of groups. Governors of almshouses, professors and their students, civic guards, all were anxious for collective immortality. Frans Hals was one of the great masters of both individual and group portraiture, a fact somewhat obscured by his popular renown as the painter of *The Laughing Cavalier*, and by the even greater fame of Rembrandt.

Rembrandt van Rijn (1606–69) is the greatest Dutch painter, and in many people's opinion the greatest painter of all time. He was for some years a successful and prosperous artist in Amsterdam, where he painted such group portraits as *The Anatomy Lesson of Dr Tulp* and the famous *Night Watch*. In *The Night Watch* the civic guardsmen emerge from darkness into warm light; they are not, as in earlier Dutch painting, a static group but an informal party of strongly characterised individuals on the march. Later, Rembrandt developed an increasingly introspective art that found little public favour and led him into bankruptcy; he must surely be the first artist consciously to pursue his private vision without patronage or public approval—a situation that was to become commonplace in the 19th century. Rembrandt is unavoidably described in terms of his humanity and deep insight into the soul of man. His art is accurate and compassionate, passing no judgments; descriptive rather than dramatic; one in which personality is explored in repose rather than in action. He was his own favourite subject, and his scores of self-portraits form a unique record of the progress of years and increasing perplexities. In *Bathsheba* [**111**] and other Biblical paintings the characters are ordinary men and women like those around him. Unlike Caravaggio [**106**], he avoids the dramatic. His use of light and shade is subservient to the quieter mood of the scene, and Bathsheba is shown not in a state of agitation but after she has taken in the contents of King David's letter; her mood seems to be a mixture of resignation and mild anticipation. The domestic setting, with the serving-woman drying Bathsheba's feet, underlines the fact that this is a human, not a heroic or mythical event.

Like his great contemporaries Rubens and Velasquez,

109 Wren: St Paul's cathedral, London.
110 Vermeer: The Painter in his Studio. Kunsthistorisches Museum, Vienna.

Rembrandt used an increasingly free brushwork–that is, strokes visible to the eye, employed to create softer and less defined forms as played upon by the light. By contrast Jan Vermeer of Delft created forms that have a great distinctness despite the mellow light in which they are bathed. His subject-matter is undramatically domestic–a woman pouring water from a jug, a lace-maker, the artist himself in his studio [110]–but freezing the moment gives the scene a feeling of timeless significance.

The Spanish painter Diego Velasquez was an almost exact contemporary of Rembrandt. Unlike the Dutch master, there seems to be no conflict between his development as an artist and his career as court painter to the king of Spain. Though he painted historical setpieces such as *The Surrender of Breda*, and the famous nude *Rokeby Venus*, his most remarkable works are probably his portraits. These are outwardly formal, though obviously truthful; the painting of Philip IV

[112] is scarcely flattering, and in other Velasquez portraits Philip's jutting Habsburg jaw looks positively grotesque. But the painter's honesty went further and deeper than this: his kings and popes are uneasy, all-too-human figures, vaguely conscious of their inability to live up to the authority proclaimed by their clothing. Philip, in his shiny armour, clutching his baton, some-how fails completely to match up to a heroically determined figure like his ancestor Charles V as Titian saw him [80].

These psychological profundities are largely absent from the paintings of the Fleming Peter Paul Rubens, whose swirling compositions, energetic execution and rich colour reveal the brighter, more self-confident side of Baroque art. Rubens was the most wealthy, successful and travelled of 17th-century artists. He carried out several diplomatic missions for his patrons, had ample opportunity to study the paintings of the Italian masters in Rome, met Velasquez in Spain and worked

III Rembrandt: Bathsheba. Louvre, Paris.

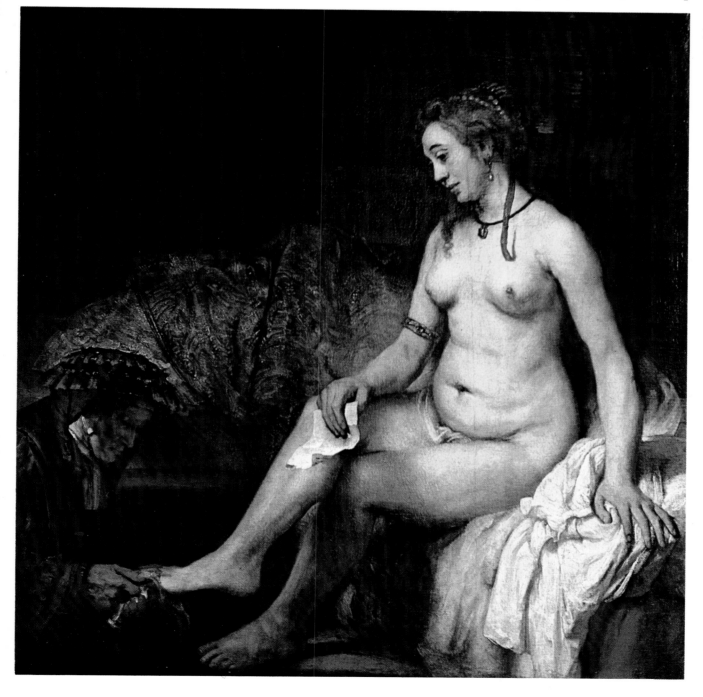

for Charles I in England. As court painter in Antwerp he was deluged with commissions from Flanders and other countries, and ran a workshop which turned out huge numbers of mythological and religious paintings, as well as portraits and series of decorative paintings celebrating royal power. Often he only sketched out and touched up works, the rest being done by his scores of assistants; one of these, Anthony van Dyck, came to England and began the long English tradition of aristocratic portraiture.

Rubens' art, like his life, exudes glowing vitality. His epic paintings pulsate with dynamic rhythms, and he uses paint in a wholly new way to convey not only the colour but the feel of flesh, textures, armour and landscape. The vitality comes through even where there is no action, as in this double portrait of Hélène Fourment and her son [113].

In the early 18th century a lighter mood spread through Europe. In France there was a reaction against the oppressive and public magnificence of Louis XIV's court, shown in a preference for intimate interiors decorated in the new Rococo style–a tamed Baroque with gentler curves, lighter colours and less obtrusive decoration. The elegant furniture produced throughout the century by French craftsmen was another symptom of the urge to live in a comfortable civilised private way.

The Rococo mood is escapist–paradoxically, since it coincides with the beginning of the Enlightenment or Age of Reason, when writers like Voltaire began to attack prejudice and injustice. In Antoine Watteau's paintings the characters move about in a hazy aristocratic fairyland, making love, listening to music or, as here, enjoying *The Pleasures of the Ball* [116]; but there is always a tinge of sadness and nostalgia. Later French Rococo painting tends to be rather coyly erotic without recapturing either the robustness of Rubens or the profundity of Watteau.

The delicacy of porcelain, which Europeans had just discovered how to make, was entirely suited to the new mood. Amorous shepherds and shepherdesses vied in

112

112 Velasquez: Philip IV on Horseback. Prado, Madrid.

113 Rubens: Hélène Fourment and Her Son. Pinakothek, Munich.

114 Harlequin and Columbine, modelled in porcelain by Bustelli at the Nymphenburg porcelain factory. Bayerisches Nationalmuseum, Munich.

114

popularity with figures from the gay Italian *commedia dell'arte* theatre, of which the Harlequin and Columbine [**114**], modelled by Franz Anton Bustelli at the Nymphenburg factory in Bavaria, are stock characters. Rulers of the many German states imitated French Rococo just as they had imitated Versailles, and in south Germany and Austria a splendid church architecture was created in which, as at Ottobeuren [**117**], stunning effects are obtained by combining the Baroque sense of space with the lightness and delicacy of Rococo decoration. The greatest decorative painter of the age was the Venetian Giambattista Tiepolo, in whose work radiant blue skies and sunlit clouds dominate the grand spectacle that would have engrossed Rubens's attention. The other important Italian painters were also Venetians, notably Canaletto and Guardi, famous for their views of the city.

In the middle of the 18th century there was a vogue for a less aristocratic and more realistic painting. In France J. B. S. Chardin's quiet still-lifes and domestic interiors were reminiscent of Dutch art. The enor-mously popular Greuze painted moralistic and senti-mental scenes of a kind usually associated with the Victorians.

Meanwhile in England William Hogarth produced series of paintings in which the moralising had a grotesque touch and a sharp edge of social observation. *The Rake's Progress*, *The Harlot's Progress* and others satirise the selfdestructive follies of men and women – and incidentally give the moralist a chance to show the squalid but racy underside of London life. The public enjoyed it all immensely, and the engravings that Hogarth made from his paintings were sold by the thousand. *The Countess's Dressing-Room* [**115**] is a catalogue of high-class frivolities and vices, the scattered playing-cards and erotic paintings suggesting the activities Hogarth was unable to work into an already crammed picture.

Hogarth's true successors were caricaturists such as Gillray and Rowlandson. In other branches of art, realism gave way to yet another style inspired by ad-miration of ancient Greece and Rome.

115 Hogarth: The Countess's Dressing-
Room. National Gallery, London.

116 Watteau: The Pleasures of the Ball.
Dulwich College Picture Gallery, London.

117 Interior of the abbey church at
Ottobeuren, Bavaria.

Neo-Classical and Romantic Art

The charming English country houses of the early 18th century were imitations of an imitation, based on Andrea Palladio's Renaissance versions of Roman villas. Later in the century English and French artists reacted against the frivolities of the Rococo by trying to create a more 'serious' art, with straight lines and severe curves, that took in all the branches of architecture and also interior decoration and sculpture. For this they looked directly to Antiquity, intending to create a New (Neo-) Classicism, though they never used the term. (Here 'Classical' means not 5th-century BC Greece but Greco-Roman culture as a whole.) They also tried to be much more faithful to their models, inspired by the more extensive and accurate information which had become available. Scholarship and travel had revealed new aspects of Antique art, and the excavation of Pompeii and Herculaneum was providing a clearer picture of life in late Roman times. Even more important was what can only be called the rediscovery of Greek art. Visitors to Paestum and Athens came to realise that Greek art and architecture had distinctive characteristics – and that, for example, the arches, domes and heavy decoration of Roman buildings, held up as models of 'Classicism' since the Renaissance, were nothing of the sort. Greek styles – and especially the austere Doric order – appealed to the new taste for sobriety and led to the launching of a separate 'Greek revival'. All in all, a great variety of buildings in Greek and Roman styles were put up in the 18th and 19th centuries, ranging from country houses to great public buildings like the Panthéon in Paris and the British Museum in London. A similar development occurred in the United States, where the Palladianism of 'Colonial' architecture was followed by the Roman Neo-Classicism of Thomas Jefferson's Capitol at Richmond.

Neo-Classicism produced a particularly attractive decorative art. Its great genius was the Scottish architect Robert Adam, who took charge of the interior decoration of houses designed both by himself and by other architects. The dining-room at Saltram House [118] shows the effects that could be achieved with the new style, and also how 'unclassical' it could be. For all its columns, friezes, garlands and urns, this is not a Roman room but something fresh and delightful: a light airy interior, created from a skilful arrangement of pale colours, white plasterwork reliefs, elegant furniture and mellow paintings. Much of the pottery developed by Josiah Wedgwood at his Staffordshire factory has the same kind of feeling, and Wedgwood jasperware with applied white reliefs is still being sold all over the world by the firm that he founded.

By contrast most Neo-Classical sculpture now seems lifeless in its efforts to reproduce the calm nobility of Classical art. Painters could not be so imitative even if they wanted to, since Roman painting was still hardly known, but selfconsciously 'Roman' attitudes were struck. In Britain, history painting and paintings of heroic contemporary events became popular; *The Death of General Wolfe*, by the American-born Benjamin West sounded an appropriate imperial theme. The French artists David and Ingres made a more rigorous attempt to achieve a Neo-Classical style. The high moral tones, severe lines and cold colours of David's *Oath of the Horatii* [119] started a whole cult of republican virtue in France that was soon to be translated into political fact by the Revolution. The heroic, glorifying passion and energy, passes over easily into the Romantic. David was an ardent supporter of the Revolution, and later of Napoleon; and as the chronicler of an epic age in such paintings as *The Death of Marat* and *Bonaparte Crossing the Alps* he can only be regarded as a political Romantic.

The Romantic movement was a European revolt against the Age of Reason and Classicism, with its analytical spirit and passion for 'rules' in the arts. A

118

craving for a new style went far back into the 18th century, especially in England, showing itself at first in an only half-serious cult of exotic arts and of untamed nature. *Chinoiserie*, a confused mixture of 'Oriental' designs, appeared in some of the furniture of the cabinetmaker Thomas Chippendale, and in the pagoda at Kew built by the Neo-Classical architect Sir William Chambers. Horace Walpole started a fashion for the mock-medieval by writing the novel *The Castle of Otranto* and having a small 'Gothick' house, Strawberry Hill, built for him at Twickenham, near London. Connoisseurs cultivated a taste for landscapes that they themselves described as 'picturesque', and the 'natural' English garden replaced the formal French one.

By the end of the century Romanticism had developed into a revolutionary new way of seeing, feeling and living. The Romantics put intensity of emotion above all rules, and sought it outside the everyday—in nature, childhood, the mysterious and strange, the sensational and exotic.

Romantic love of nature led to a greatly increased appreciation of landscape subjects, though landscape painting had already been practised as an independent

118 The dining-room at Saltram House, Devonshire, designed by Robert Adam.

119 David: The Oath of the Horatii. Louvre, Paris.

120

121

art by the 17th-century Dutch masters and the Frenchman Claude Lorrain. In the 18th century Thomas Gainsborough painted English scenes with a picturesque feathery touch. He was also a commercially successful portraitist, giving his well-born sitters a distinction never quite achieved by his great rival Sir Joshua Reynolds. Both sides of his work are represented in *Mr and Mrs Andrews* [120]. The aloof lounging husband has apparently taken a break from his shooting in a rather condescending spirit; behind the couple the peaceful English countryside stretches into the distance. The overwhelming impression created is of a social and

120 Gainsborough: Mr and Mrs Andrews. National Gallery, London.

121 Constable: Weymouth Bay. National Gallery, London.

122 Goya: Saturn Eating One of His Children. Prado, Madrid.

122

natural order destined to last for ever. Taken over into the next century in a more scientific spirit by John Constable [121] and the French Barbizon school, landscape was one of the most important subjects for painters until well into the 20th century.

Like David, the Spanish artist Francisco de Goya lived through the Revolutionary and Napoleonic period. Beginning as a decorative painter and Rococo tapestry designer for the court, he developed into an artist of tremendous power and range. He painted cruelly revealing portraits of his royal masters, and made paintings and engravings of atrocities and executions carried out by both sides in the Peninsular War, creating a universe of madness and horror that contradicts the heroic vision of David. And as a satirist with a genius for the grotesque and fantastic, he mocked the fads and follies of his contemporaries. Goya's expressionism reached its climax in decorations for his own house, painted when he was old, isolated and deaf. In *Saturn Eating One of His Children* [122] the horror seems to rise out of the human soul; this astonishing work could well be a cry of despair uttered by an artist of our own time, such as Francis Bacon.

Romantic feeling assumed many forms. The English poet William Blake made coloured engravings of an intense visionary quality that is also found in his follower, Samuel Palmer. In Germany, Caspar David Friedrich painted mysterious landscapes with ruins and gnarled trees, and the Nazarenes, led by Johann Friedrich Overbeck, attempted to revive German religious art in a 'medieval' spirit that later influenced the English Pre-Raphaelites. Eugène Delacroix and the French Romantics were generally more extroverted. Delacroix's *Liberty Leading the People* celebrates the revolution of 1830; *The Death of Sardanapalus* [124] combines grandiose historical fiction with an erotico-sadistic element found in a great deal of Romantic art; and *The Women of Algiers* is an exercise in colourful exoticism. In Géricault's *Raft of the Medusa* the intention was realistic, but his desperate survivors of a wreck, bathed in ghastly yellow light, are in fact experienced as Romantically sensational.

Joseph Mallord William Turner made a real break with the past in style as well as in mood. His paintings of historical events and land- and seascapes are filled with a Romantic excitement, with movement and striking effects; and in his late work he achieved them by an amazingly daring use of paint. He is the master of atmospheric effects, and especially of a light that causes forms to melt into one another. In his paintings nature is always greater than man, either enveloping him in the misty golden light of a peaceful landscape [123] or stormily tossing him about between sea and sky. This is like nothing else we have seen so far in this book in the free handling of paint, anticipating the Impressionism of a few years later, and even approaching pure abstraction.

123 Turner: Norham Castle. Tate Gallery,
London.

124 Delacroix: The Death of Sardanapalus.
Louvre, Paris.

125 Courbet: Funeral at Ornans. Louvre, Paris.

123

124

Impressionism and After

The 19th century began the age of revolutionary experiment in art. New schools, movements and styles multiplied, and have continued to multiply ever since. All this is part of the modern spirit, and very much like what has happened in politics, literature and ideas; but it also had a great deal to do with the changed situation of the artist.

In the past artists had usually worked for great patrons—for Church or king or nobles. They had carried out set commissions—to paint a portrait or decorate a palace—and found a limited but sufficient freedom in enlightened patronage. Now they were dependent on the 'general public'—in practice a moneyed middle class that was cautious, conventional and suspicious of anything that might not be 'respectable'. Public taste was for historical narrative, cosy domestic scenes and mythological subjects spiced with a concealed eroticism. Nowadays this kind of art is called 'academic' because it was given a semi-official seal of approval by institutions such as the British Royal Academy and the Salon in Paris.

In this atmosphere, artists with new ideas learned to go their own way even if they failed to win over the public. So was born the modern idea of the *avant-garde* —the pioneering 'vanguard' of artists who could expect recognition only (if at all) after years of struggle.

This unheard-of freedom was acquired at the cost of alienation from society; and the total rejection of the more extreme and singleminded—Gauguin, van Gogh— started the quite modern idea of the artist as misfit or outcast.

In the 1850s two groups attempted to break with academic tradition: the Realists in France and the Pre-Raphaelites in Britain. In his *Funeral at Ornans* [125] Gustave Courbet tried to show a peasant funeral as it really was, without idealising or sentimentalising it. The mourners are in their Sunday best, but they have the rugged faces and worn hands of peasants. The occasion itself is a perfunctory one, despite the sniffling women; the acolytes are no more interested in what is going on than the dog is. The Pre-Raphaelites—Dante Gabriel Rossetti, Holman Hunt, Sir John Millais— aimed to recover a sense of devotional freshness that they believed had been lost through the idealisations of Raphael and his school. Some Pre-Raphaelite paintings are heavily symbolic; some—probably the ones most people now like best—are decorative pieces in vibrant colours.

Realism and symbolism had a considerable impact in the 19th century, but in the long term the works of Edouard Manet were more important. *Olympia* [126] is a revolutionary picture. Like the Byzantine artists

25

discussed on page 32, Manet is not interested in 'photographic' realism: the painting is flat and two-dimensional, the tones are dark, the range of colours is limited, and little use is made of shadow and shades of colour. It is another step towards the idea that a work of art is not a picture of reality but an independent arrangement of shapes and colours. The subject gave as much offence as the treatment. It is modern, and shockingly modern at that: the girl is no rosy inviting nude trailing scanty 'classical' draperies, but a dispassionate figure whose aura of cool commercial sex is emphasised by her choker and shoes.

Manet was the first great painter to work outside the academy system. In 1863, the year he painted *Olympia*, he exhibited at the Salon des Refusés, organised to show works rejected by the official Salon. From this time *avant-garde* artists began to organise their own exhibitions and sell through far-sighted art dealers, a procedure that allowed them gradually to create their own public. Paris now became the chief centre of modern art, attracting painters and sculptors from all over Europe and America; the domination of the 'School of Paris' lasted unbroken down to the Second World War.

The first coherent group to exhibit together were the Impressionists in the 1870s. 'Impressionism' comes from *Impression–Sunrise*, exhibited by Claude Monet in 1874; the name was first used to ridicule Monet and his friends Sisley, Pissarro, Renoir and Degas. Ironically the bright spontaneous pictures of the Impressionists are almost certainly the paintings ordinary people know and like best. Theirs is an art of the open air, executed on the spot to capture fleeting atmospheric effects, and above all the play of light. Instead of the solid forms of studio-made landscapes, they used blobs of colour pure; even the shadows are not conventionally black but coloured, as they are in nature.

Monet was the most unswerving of the Impressionists. A picture like *Springtime* [127] approaches the Impressionist ideal, untouched by sentimentality, moral message or even the artist's feeling about what he is looking at. Monet often painted the same subject again and again under different atmospheric conditions, and by the end of his life (he died in 1926) was making close-up studies of waterlilies that verge on abstraction.

Mood is much more important in Pierre Auguste Renoir's work. Renoir was a painter of people – of women dressed and undressed, and of townspeople lounging in cafés or, as in *The Swing* [128], relaxing in the park. This shows his feathery touch, and a mastery of dappled light effects that gives a wonderful texture and sheen to everything in the picture.

The next generation began to follow different paths.

126 Manet: Olympia. Musée de l'Impressionnisme, Paris.
127 Monet: Springtime. Nationalgalerie, West Berlin.

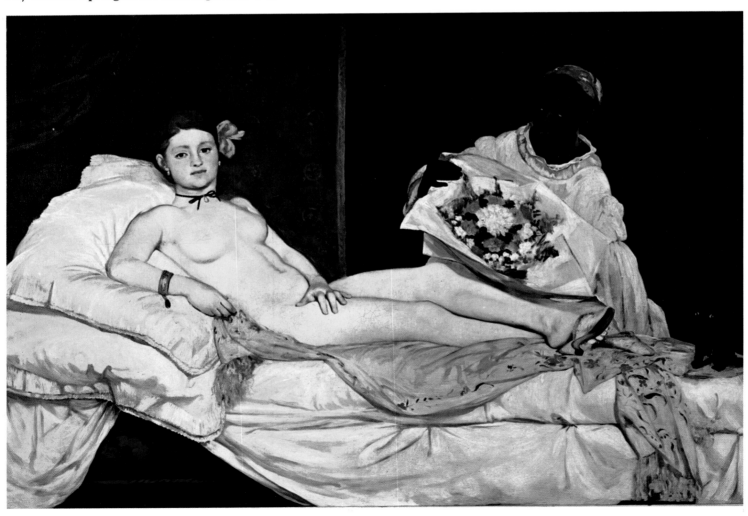

126

In paintings such as *Sunday Afternoon on the Island of the Grande Jatte* [129], Georges Seurat took the Impressionist technique a stage further in a scientific spirit, applying his colours in tiny dots. The dots making up a particular subject—grass, water, clothing—are not all one colour, but a mixture calculated to give a new and brilliant colour or subtle shading. This technique is called *pointillisme* or divisionism. But Seurat uses the technique in a completely different spirit from the Impressionists, creating solid, well-defined forms and an impressively elaborate overall design. The peaceful family pleasures of the *Grande Jatte* have a still timeless quality that is far removed from the 'uncomposed' spontaneous look of a Monet. For want of a better term, Seurat and his followers have been labelled 'Neo-Impressionists'.

Vincent van Gogh's life has become part of the modern legend of the artist. The son of a Dutch pastor, he was a lonely, tormented man who failed to gain any sort of acceptance in the world—from women, or as an evangelist in a Belgian mining village, or as an artist. He began to find himself only in his thirties; and after intermittent bouts of insanity he shot himself at the age of thirty-seven. All the paintings on which his fame rests were done in the last three years of his life. The portrait of Dr Gachet [130] is typical in its intense

colours, simplified forms and swirling lines, which add a feeling of profound disturbance to the sorrow and disillusion shown on the doctor's face. Van Gogh's is a visionary art in which a sunflower, a chair, a starry night or a sea of corn blaze with strange life, seen through the eyes of a man shadowed by insanity but also more than sane. As an artist van Gogh's greatest originality lies in the handling of the paint itself, piled on with thick heavy repeated brush-strokes, often to a point where it stands out from the picture surface like a massy relief. The 'sculptural' quality of paint, first shown by van Gogh, was to be exploited still more radically by some of the great artists of the twentieth century.

Paul Gauguin's legend complements van Gogh's: he was the stockbroker of forty who gave up everything to paint, rejected respectable society, and at last deserted civilisation for the South Seas. But Gauguin's art has nothing of van Gogh's violence of statement: his Tahitian and Marquesan women are still enigmatic figures, flatly presented and defined by firm black outlines. *Nevermore* [131] has a good deal in common with Manet's *Olympia* [126] and seems to have been directly inspired by it; but the differences are just as important. Gauguin liked to hint that his paintings carried profound statements about life, usually by

127

129 Seurat: Sunday Afternoon on the Island of the Grande Jatte. Art Institute, Chicago (Helen Birch Bartlett Memorial Collection).

130 Van Gogh: Dr Gachet. Musée de l'Impressionnisme, Paris.

giving them sententious titles. *Nevermore* is particularly literary: the word is the refrain croaked by the raven in Edgar Allan Poe's poem, driving home the finality of separation from a dead lover; Gauguin even puts the raven into the picture. He was also much more of a decorative artist than his predecessors, sprinkling the bed and walls with plants and making a pattern of curves from the girl's body and the headboard. Here it all works magnificently. The decoration only points out our uneasy awareness of the girl's malaise, and the close walls and absorbed background figures create an oppressive atmosphere of whispered secrets.

Paul Cézanne is often classified with Seurat, van Gogh and Gauguin as a 'Post-Impressionist'—a term which more or less admits that all these painters had in common was their development away from Impressionism. In the 1870s he absorbed Impressionist techniques and exhibited with the group, but he became dissatisfied with the way in which Impressionist paintings dissolved solid objects in strong light. He returned to live in his native Aix, and in the 1880s

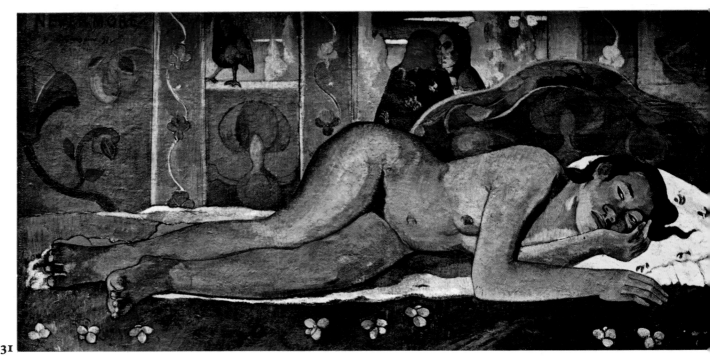

131

132

133

131 Gauguin: Nevermore. Courtauld Institute Galleries, London.

132 Cézanne: The Little Bridge, Mennecy. Louvre, Paris.

133 Toulouse-Lautrec: Divan Japonais. Colour lithograph. Musée Toulouse-Lautrec, Albi.

developed a revolutionary approach to painting that went unrecognised until a few years before his death in 1906. In paintings like *The Little Bridge, Mennecy* [**132**] he kept the bright colours of the Impressionist palette but used them to emphasise the solidity of things. Reflections in the water are as solid as the trees or the bridge itself, painted with emphatic strokes that reinforce the concrete reality of the picture surface and form part of its total organisation. This is not patterning or decoration or expressionism, but a revelation of the structure of things. More than any other painter, Cézanne was to give the lead to artists in the early 20th century.

Henri de Toulouse-Lautrec's *Divan Japonais* [**133**] does just what a good poster should—catches the attention and delivers its message in a few seconds. Lautrec was a master at conveying movements and atmosphere with a few strokes of the pen or brush; the two-dimensional treatment and large areas of flat bold colour add a strongly patterned effect. The influence of Japanese prints is particularly strong here (see page 78), but it was also felt by most French painters after 1850, including Edgar Degas and Manet. Lautrec used similar techniques to capture the spirit of Parisian life in the 1890s, painting the music hall and its stars, the circus, the brothel and the racetrack.

Auguste Rodin began the liberation of sculpture from insipid academic styles, introducing drama and emotional intensity. Instead of smooth rounded forms he created broken surfaces which dramatically reflect the changing play of light. The tense impassioned figures of *Romeo and Juliet* [**134**] are wound about each other with erotic directness, and the 'half-finished' look heightens the impression of passion and energy, with the figures apparently struggling out of unworked bronze. We are made conscious of the bronze just as we are made conscious of the paint in a van Gogh picture.

Despite the changes in painting and sculpture, only one new general style of decoration was introduced in the 19th century. This was Art Nouveau, which broke upon the 1890s in sinuous flowing lines, usually variations on lush elongated plant forms. Hector Guimard's Paris underground (Métro) entrances [**135**] are a striking example of Art Nouveau applied to wrought iron; apart from the long-stemmed drooping flowers, notice the rubbery organic quality of the rest of the ironwork. Art Nouveau decoration was applied to buildings, furniture and other objects, but it was perhaps most effective of all in glass, in which stems and bulbs lent themselves to the creation of superb floral objects by such makers as Louis Tiffany in New York and Emile Gallé at Nancy in France. Art Nouveau owed a good deal to the British 'Arts and Crafts' movement and the work of the poet-designer William Morris, who sought to revive handicrafts destroyed by machine mass-production. But Art Nouveau was more commercially oriented and more distinctively a style. The 'Art Nouveau line' crops up in all sorts of places—in Gauguin's *Nevermore* [**131**] (look at the plant on the left-hand side of the wall!) as well as in the decadent ink drawings of Aubrey Beardsley.

In architecture the 19th century was an era of revivals. Instead of new styles the great styles of the past were adapted with more or less feeling for appropriateness: there were Greek museums, Gothic railway stations, Renaissance banks and Baroque opera-houses. The 'style' of such a building really amounted to a layer of (say) Gothic decoration plastered over a structure intended for modern purposes, concealing or distorting the shapes naturally arising out of such purposes. That is why the most interesting 19th-century structures are often engineering works such as bridges and docks, which mave no applied 'style' because they were not thought of as 'art'. Joseph Paxton's vast iron and glass Crystal Palace in London, and Gustave Eiffel's famous iron tower in Paris, fall into the same category, revealing the possibilities of new materials and building on a new scale. Among architects proper, the breakthrough began in the 1890s, when the Chicago architect Louis H. Sullivan built office blocks on the principle that 'form follows function': in other words, a beautiful building is one that does its job with maximum efficiency, and can be seen to be doing it. The Guaranty Building [136] in Buffalo is an office block, not a temple, despite the sprinkling of Art Nouveau ornament—a severe, steel-framed grid structure with regular window spaces. Sullivan's Functionalism was to become one of the central ideas of modern architecture, with repercussions that are still being felt all over the world.

134 Rodin: Romeo and Juliet. Musée Rodin, Paris.
135 Hector Guimard: Metro entrance, Paris.
136 Sullivan: Guaranty Building, Buffalo.

134

135

The Beginnings of Modern Art

The 20th century was only five years old when Parisians were startled by Salon paintings in hectic bright non-realistic colours. A hostile critic talked of *fauves* ('wild beasts'), and the name stuck. Matisse's portrait of Madame Matisse (*The Green Stripe*) [137] is certainly aggressive in its colours and its apparently crude brushwork and modelling; neither Gauguin nor van Gogh could have painted it, though Matisse took a great deal from both. After the Fauves went their separate ways – around 1907 – Matisse, the leader, remained one of the great figures of modern art. Outside his Fauve period he was concerned to create a serene untroubled art, rarely touching on the darker side of life; and he also developed a strong taste for decoration. Harmony and brightness prevail even in his last works – painted pieces of paper cut up, arranged and pasted down – which were done when he was physically unable to paint.

The influence of Cézanne largely ended the Fauvist fashion. Pablo Picasso, a Spanish painter working in Paris, took as a starting point Cézanne's remark that everything in Nature could be reduced to three shapes, the cylinder, the sphere and the cone. Picasso's *Demoiselles d'Avignon* [140] is an extraordinary picture for its time (1907) and filled with a powerful barbaric feeling. This stems from Picasso's study of African masks, most openly shown in the women's faces – the first time, incidentally, that primitive works had been taken seriously by Europeans as art. But its most revolutionary feature is the way in which the women, the drapery and the vague background are reduced to near-geometrical forms. The mask/face of the squatting figure combines a full-face view with a profile; it may remind us of a similar combination in Egyptian painting (see page 16), but its importance for the future lay in breaking down the object shown into a number of planes or facets – including facets that could not all be seen from one angle.

Picasso was soon joined by Georges Braque, and the two between them created the most influential of all modern styles, Cubism. Mostly they painted in the dullest of colours, as if to emphasise that they were concerned only with the relationship between the shapes in their pictures. Eventually the breaking up of reality into geometrical facets reached a point at which the subject of a picture could only be picked out with some effort. Braque's *Still-Life with Fish* [138] is a good

example of this most austere phase of the style.

Cubism was developed by Juan Gris, and by Ferdinand Léger and Robert Delaunay, who created new versions in which colour was a dynamic element; but after the First World War the movement lost much of its impetus. By that time, however, its influence had become enormous, as we shall see when we come to examine later movements.

The other great pre-1914 movement was Expressionism. This, as we have seen, is a permanent tendency in art: the impulse to distort 'reality' to express emotion runs from the Venus of Savignano [2] to van Gogh [130]. But in the 20th century it has been one of the main currents in art, providing an alternative outlet to highly intellectual styles such as Cubism. The variety has been amazing, since Expressionists have generally worked outside groups, each fashioning his personal vision. The great names of the period up to 1945 include the painters Edvard Munch, Georges Rouault, Oskar Kokoschka, George Grosz, Marc Chagall and Stanley Spencer, and the sculptors Ossip Zadkine and Jacob Epstein. Many other artists, for example Picasso and Matisse, have worked in an Expressionist style at some stage in their careers.

But in the years before 1914 there was one Expressionist group that was close-knit by any standards. The German *Die Brücke* (Bridge) group was contemporary with the Fauves in Paris, but produced a far more emotionally charged, even neurotic, art. Ernst Ludwig Kirchner's *Artist and Model* [139] has a starkness and sense of unease never found in Matisse; the violent raw colours and 'crude' forms transform the harmless traditional subject into a tense, vaguely sinister scene.

Cubism led in a quite different direction. Picasso stuck pieces of rope, paper and other items on to his canvases, creating a new art: the collage. He even put together various objects to make three-dimensional sculptures – what are now known as 'assemblages'. This was putting into practice a theory that had been current since the 1890s: that a work of art was not a 'mirror held up to Nature' but an arrangement of shapes and colours – a new, independently interesting object, not a copy of an old one.

The Cubists themselves never took this line of thought to its logical conclusion: their works always include some kind of recognisable object from the real world. But they were soon followed by artists who made completely abstract works, intended to be looked at without any thought of what they represented or even what they 'meant'. The pioneers were a Russian, Wassily Kandinsky, and a Dutchman, Piet Mondrian. Some people claim that Kandinsky painted the first abstract picture around 1910; others argue that even these were not quite 'pure', and that Mondrian was first. It hardly matters now. What is important is that by 1920 Mondrian was painting pictures like the one shown here [141]. This is pure abstraction, as 'meaning-

Matisse: Madame Matisse ('The Green Stripe'). Royal
Museum of Fine Arts, Copenhagen.

138 Braque: Still-life with Fish. Tate Gallery, London.

139 Kirchner: The Artist and Model. Kunsthalle, Hamburg.

140 Picasso: Les Demoiselles d'Avignon. Museum of Modern Art, New York (acquired through the Lillie P. Bliss Bequest).

138

13

less' as a seashell or a flower. (It did, it is true, have some kind of mystical significance for Mondrian, but that has not concerned the rest of us.) Mondrian limited himself to the three primary colours (red, yellow, blue) and the three non-colours (black, white, grey), and until the last years of his life he enclosed areas of pure colour in rectangular grid structures like this one. He was supremely successful in ringing the changes on these few elements, producing a simple, serene and harmonious art.

Nothing could be further from this than Dada and Surrealism. Dada started in 1916 among a group of artists who had come to Switzerland to escape from the war. They expressed their disillusion with civilisation and its bloodstained 'progress' by creating an outrageously irreverent and wildly zestful anti-art. Marcel Duchamp made two typical Dadaist gestures, putting a urinal on exhibition and drawing moustaches on a reproduction of the *Mona Lisa*.

In the 1920s Dada merged with Surrealism. The Surrealists, led by the poet André Breton, took over the irrationalism of the Dadaists and—strange as it may sound—turned it into an intellectual programme. By this time the psychoanalytical theories of Sigmund Freud had become widely known and provided justification for an art of the unconscious that recorded dreams and irrationally associated images. Hence the elephant like a boiler in Max Ernst's *Elephant of the Celebes*, the dripping watches in Salvador Dali's *Persistence of Memory*, the train steaming out of the fireplace in René Magritte's *Time Transfixed* [143]. Surrealism was a liberating movement that brought a new imagination and invention into art. And not just art: a careful look through almost any magazine will turn up at least one 'Surrealist' advertisement or cartoon.

So much happened in art during the 20th century that it seems natural to concentrate on styles and movements. This is a useful way of approaching the subject,

providing we remember that it does not exhaust it. Every artist of real worth creates his personal interpretation of a style, and some absorb one style and then move on to another. Picasso is an outstanding example: he is the most versatile as well as the most famous of 20th-century artists.

By contrast Paul Klee is one of those artists who cannot be fitted into any category. A painting like *Fish Magic* [**145**], with its fish and flowers and clock floating in the same element, obviously has a good deal in common with Surrealism; but its whole feeling is one of childlike freshness and gentle joyful play, not of unconscious compulsions. The childlike is always strong in Klee's work; he liked to 'take a line for a walk', perhaps starting from a doodle and allowing the picture to form and grow as he painted. He succeeded so well that even his most imaginative or fantastic paintings seem entirely natural.

After the First World War many artists believed that a new world could be built on the ruins of the old.

141 Mondrian: Composition with Red, Yellow and Blue. Alfred Roth Collection, Zürich.

142 Le Corbusier: Villa Savoye, Poissy.

143 Magritte: Time Transfixed. Edward James Foundation, on loan to the Tate Gallery, London.

144 Chair designed by Marcel Breuer. Museum of Modern Art, New York.

The Surrealists hoped to do it by liberating the unconscious; designers and artists naturally looked to technology. The Dutch De Stijl group created highly effective and efficient buildings and furniture, using Mondrian's limited range of colours and rectangles [141]. The Bauhaus in Germany had a much wider impact. This school of design, founded at Weimar in 1919, was run by the architect Walter Gropius, who insisted that design must be geared to mass-production techniques. The textile designer as well as the architect was taught to think of his work as part of a total design for home or factory that must be practical and economical–made for mass use, not as a luxury item for one person. The chair [144] designed by the Bauhaus-trained Marcel Breuer shows how much we owe to Gropius's teaching. The material is modern (chromium-plated steel) and the chair itself is light, simple, elegant and eminently practical; it is in fact the prototype for the stacking chair now found almost everywhere.

Architects also wanted to use technology to make a better society, and in the 1920s there were many projects for large-scale low-cost housing for workers and 'cities of the future' for everybody. The new Bauhaus building at Dessau (1926), designed by Gropius, seemed to point the way forward. Modern materials such as concrete and glass were to be used to create more or less standardised rational efficient buildings free from ornament. Since technology and Functionalism are international, this would be the 'International Style'. In fact, between the two World Wars it was confined to western Europe; and realisation of its social ideals was largely frustrated by the Depression.

Most International Style buildings actually put up before the Second World War were private houses like Le Corbusier's Villa Savoye at Poissy [142]. This is both typical and beautiful, with its clean undecorated geometrical shapes, flat roof, long strip windows and stilts to increase the usable outside space on the ground floor. Le Corbusier was the great theoretician of modern architecture, with his own system of proportions and ambitious ideas of city planning. One was to house people in great blocks of flats like miniature cities; in these, privacy could be preserved and communal services provided, leaving large surrounding areas free for grass, flowers and trees. Le Corbusier had to wait until the late 1940s to put this idea into practice, and it has now become one of the most important ways of coping with the overcrowding and ugly noisy environment of town life. Le Corbusier's contemporary, the German architect Mies van der Rohe, was designing projects for glass skyscrapers in 1919, but between the wars he built no more than a handful of private houses. He too was to reach full stature after 1945 [155].

The third of the great modern architects was the American Frank Lloyd Wright, one of those difficult

geniuses who go their own way regardless of fashion—
even revolutionary fashion. Wright was a good many
years older than Le Corbusier and Mies. He was a
pupil of Sullivan, and his work before 1914 was one of
the sources of the International Style. But he had no
time at all for its town-bred anonymity. The Villa
Savoye [142] is what Le Corbusier called 'a machine
for living in', icily separate from nature and dominating
it. Wright wanted an 'organic' architecture which
would be like part of the landscape, and he used local
materials and advanced building techniques to create it.
His Kaufmann House [146] of 1936 is like an outcrop
of rock, jutting out over the waterfall. Inside, a massive
boulder forms the hearth of the living area. Instead of
completely separate enclosed rooms, the interior is
basically a single unit of space—the now familiar 'open
plan'—with varied treatment of the individual subordin-
ate areas.

Sculpture in the early 20th century tended to follow
the paths blazed by painters. Cubism was taken over
into sculpture by Alexander Archipenko and Jacques
Lipchitz, and Expressionism and Surrealism were also
important. More original were the Russian Con-
structivists, whose radical design ideas had some
influence on the development of the Bauhaus. Con-
structivist sculptors like Naum Gabo started as

admirers of the machine and functionalism, but they
gradually moved towards a new form of abstract art—
'constructions' of materials such as metal, glass and
plastic that did not fill space with solid objects in the
traditional way.

The Rumanian sculptor Constantin Brancusi kept
the sculptural quality of mass but simplified his forms—
so that, for example, a torso or a bird became polished
near-abstract forms. Brancusi influenced the British
sculptor Henry Moore, now generally considered the
greatest living sculptor. Moore is above all a carver,
with a wonderful feeling for shapes and textures. He
uses the techniques of abstraction, even including
'holes' in his sculptures, but has rarely produced
completely abstract works. His preferred subjects are
reclining females like the one shown here [147], or
mother-and-child groups, which enable him to give an
added dimension to what would otherwise be superb
abstract sculpture—the dimension of primal human
feeling.

Most of the movements we have looked at were well
under way by the 1920s. The 1930s were a period in
which their consequences were worked out. This
process was interrupted by the trauma of the Second
World War which left the world radically changed,
for artists·as well as for everybody else.

46

145 Klee: Fish Magic. Philadelphia Museum of Art (Louise and Walter Arensberg Collection).

146 Frank Lloyd Wright: Kaufmann House, Bear Run, Pennsylvania.

147 Henry Moore: Reclining Figure. Tate Gallery, London.

Art Today

The boom in contemporary art began shortly after the Second World War, and has grown bigger with every year. Exhibitions of works by living artists have multiplied, and regular festivals and shows like the Venice Biennale are devoted to modern art. Painters, sculptors and architects whose work was once thought outlandish have been commissioned or subsidised by governments, industrial corporations and foundations. Instead of clinging to old and accepted styles the public –or at least the buying public–eagerly welcomes novelty and even outrage. Nothing quite like this has ever happened before. The value put on novelty for its own sake sometimes encourages pseudo-originality, but generally speaking the present-day atmosphere is highly favourable to genuine creativity.

American art has come into its own since 1945, and New York has replaced Paris as a world centre. Many artists such as Ernst and Mondrian fled from Nazi-dominated Europe to the United States, and their presence undoubtedly gave modern art a new status and popularity. But Americans did more than take over European styles: they now began to create their own.

The first of these was Abstract Expressionism, pioneered during the 1940s by Jackson Pollock. This represented a break with the rather austere rigid treatment of abstract painting; one of its main characteristics was the combination of abstraction with expressive use of paint, but Americans also developed the abstract tradition in other 'non-European' directions. Pollock was an 'action painter': he put the canvas on the floor and walked round it, splashing and dribbling paint on to it from all sides. As far as possible he worked without conscious planning or execution, so that in a sense he was more Surrealist than the Surrealists, who took their subjects from the unconscious but usually painted them with controlled artistry. In Pollock's *Number Fifteen* [148] the intricate exciting network of lines and blotches gives us a strong sense of the free spontaneous way in which it was created.

Action painting is only one side of Abstract Expressionism. Willem de Kooning uses broad sweeps of paint, made with a loaded brush, to build up heavily encrusted surfaces; he has applied the technique just as successfully to figure paintings like the fearsome *Woman* series done in the 1950s. Mark Rothko created gentler, more reflective pictures with soft vibrating masses of colour. And 'hard-edge' painters like Kenneth Noland [149] brought back the well defined forms we associate with artists like Mondrian. But with a difference: instead of a static arrangement of shapes and colours, Noland gives us a picture that changes subtly as we look at it. This use of 'optical illusion' has remained one of the outstanding features of contemporary art.

Abstract Expressionism had a world-wide influence, though its greatest exponents were Americans by

148

14

birth or adoption. British painting was long dominated by Victor Pasmore, whose lush landscapes of the 1940s gave way to cool and formal three-dimensional painted reliefs – one of many signs that the old boundaries between painting and sculpture were being broken down. Graham Sutherland painted haunting war-torn landscapes in a semi-abstract style; in recent years he has become known as a portraitist (*Sir Winston Churchill, Somerset Maugham*), and as designer of the *Christ in Glory* tapestry in Coventry cathedral. Francis Bacon is a painter in the Expressionist tradition, but specifically modern in the quality of his despair: his Popes [**150**] are like victims of the electric chair or torture chamber, strapped into their seats and screaming out in agony; the streaky lines running down the picture suggest simultaneously the haze of pain and the blast of high voltage. In other, equally nightmarish works, twisted degraded human figures drag out their lives in rooms reminiscent of the gas-chambers.

The still flourishing Pop Art movement has its roots in the 1950s, when it was pioneered by Jasper Johns and Robert Rauschenberg in America and Richard Hamilton in Britain. In the 1960s it made a tremendous impact, bringing fun, irreverence and adventure into 'serious' art, and suddenly making people aware of whole areas of daily experience that they had taken for

50

148 Jackson Pollock: Number Fifteen. Cardazzo Collection, Venice.

149 Kenneth Noland: New Light. Ulster Museum, Belfast.

150 Francis Bacon: Study after Velasquez, Portrait of Pope Innocent X. Carter Burden Collection, New York.

151 Roy Lichtenstein: Holly Solomon. Collection of Mr and Mrs Horace Solomon.

152 Claes Oldenburg: Soft Giant Drum Set. Collection of John G. Powers, Aspen, Colorado.

granted. Pop artists have abandoned the intensely personal expression of artists like Pollock and Bacon. They take their images from the commercial mass media—advertising, television, films, magazines and comics. They work directly with these images rather than creating their own versions of reality: Andy Warhol's prints of Marilyn Monroe, for example, are coloured copies of a cheesecake photograph, not portraits in the traditional sense.

Many Pop artists simply reproduce the image, relying on differences in materials and scale to produce an effect—or even simply the psychological difference that comes from looking at an advertisement as a work of art. Examples are Jasper Johns' beer cans and his canvas of the Stars and Stripes, Warhol's Campbell soups, and Roy Lichtenstein's blow-ups of single cartoon frames. But there are also other ways of using Pop styles and subjects. Lichtenstein's *Holly Solomon* [151], for example, is a painting of a real person, done in the comic-strip idiom—insipidly idealised and complete with balloon and sentimental words. And there is also a 'Neo-Dada' side to Pop, shown in the revival of photo-montage. Claes Oldenburg's *Soft Drum Set* [152] has the same disconcerting quality: instead of the taut hard-edged objects we expect, we find a squashy

collapsed heap reminiscent of garbage. The materials (vinyl stuffed with kapok) are true to the Pop taste for consumer-society modernity which, whatever our feelings about it in general, has greatly enriched art.

Op—'optical'—art became fashionable in the 1960s, though without supplanting Pop. Op artists specialise in arrangements of shapes and colours that deceive the eye, which 'sees' movements and changing relationships on what is in fact a static two-dimensional surface. *Crest* [153], by the leading British Op artist Bridget Riley, exploits these effects far more thoroughly than the hard-edge painting by Noland [149]: after you have looked at it for a few seconds it appears to flicker and flow in an uncanny way. Op is related to 'Kinetic' art, which also relies on movement for its effects— but actual movement caused by currents of air, as in Alexander Calder's mobiles, or by mechanical means.

Sculpture has been less dominated by schools and movements. An amazing variety of works has been produced, ranging from the squashed car-bodies of the French sculptor César to the sinister bird-forms of Lynn Chadwick in Britain. A particular popularity was enjoyed by sculptors who mirrored post-war anxieties— for example Germaine Richier, also French, and the

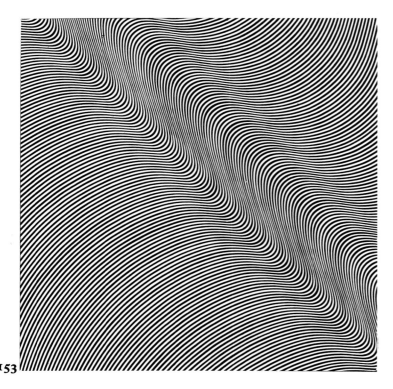

153

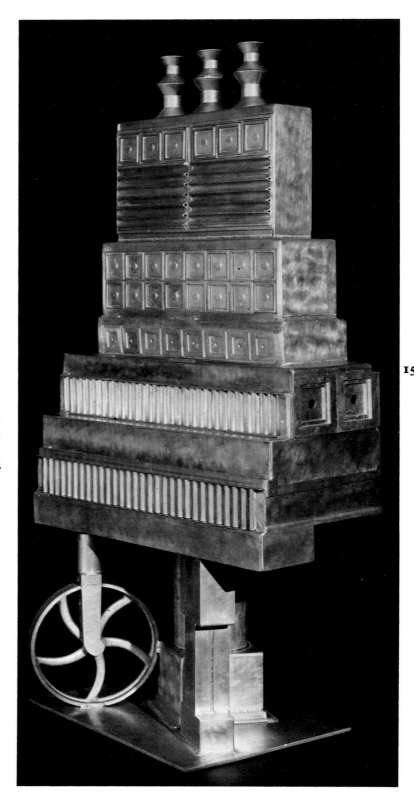

15

Swiss Alberto Giacometti, who made knobbly attenuated figures with a fraught and solitary air. Much more use has been made of iron, steel, aluminium and other metals, and 'assemblages' of readymade parts and painted reliefs have greatly widened the scope of sculpture. In Britain the art has continued to flourish; the best-known sculptors of the last few years are probably Anthony Caro and Eduardo Paolozzi. Almost all of Paolozzi's works reflect his obsession with modern technology, combined most recently with a strong influence from Pop. Paolozzi's pseudo-machines, shining with chrome or decorated with machine parts like badges, seem to have a kind of cultic significance, as if they are meant to be totems of a new religion. *The City of the Circle and the Square* [154] is like some strange keyboard instrument, but gives the chilling impression that sacrifices rather than sonatas are performed on it.

In architecture the International Style has now become world-wide, and may possibly prove to be the typical style of the 20th century. Here too the flight of Europeans from Nazism—Le Corbusier to Brazil, Gropius to England and later America—was important. The dominant influence has undoubtedly been the severe rectangular style of Mies van der Rohe, who settled just before the war in Chicago, where the steel-frame Sullivan tradition was still strong. The Seagram Building [155], which Mies completed in collaboration with Philip Johnson in 1958, is probably the climax of his achievement. This photograph shows it rising clear and clean against the night sky and emphasises the feeling of quiet luxury given by its sheathing of bronze and brown glass windows; its uncluttered beauty is brought out by the 'sacrifice' of two-thirds of the valuable New York ground space to make a 'plaza' in front of it.

Architects from Finland to Japan now work in the International Style, finding it adaptable to climate and national tradition. But some, like the American architect Paul Rudolph, have reacted against its anonymity. Le Corbusier himself went over to a more expressionistic style; his church at Ronchamp, with its great curving roof and rounded forms, has the impact of a massive piece of modern sculpture. And Buckminster Fuller's geodesic domes, which can roof vast areas, present yet another possible line of development.

In architecture, as in all the arts, the present is unclear. And the future, of course, is impossible to predict.

153 Bridget Riley: Crest. Peter Stuyvesant Foundation
Collection.

154 Paolozzi: The City of the Circle and the Square. Tate
Gallery, London.

155 Mies van der Rohe: Seagram Building, New York.

Acknowledgments

Plate 74 is reproduced by gracious permission of Her Majesty the Queen. Plate 116 is reproduced by permission of the Governors of Dulwich College Picture Gallery, and Plate 45 and the illustration on page 4 by the Board of Trinity College, Dublin. Plates 138 and 143 Rights Reserved A.D.A.G.P. Paris 1973. Plates 127, 134, 137, 140, 145 and the illustration on page 1 © by S.P.A.D.E.M. Paris

Photographs were supplied by Aerofilms, London 5; Alinari, Florence 68, 69, 70, 71, 75, 79, 104; Archaeological Survey of India 9, 30; Archives Photographiques, Paris 25, 57; Art Institute of Chicago 129; Ashmolean Museum, Oxford 35; Lala Aufsberg, Sonthofen 117; Bevilacqua, Milan 62; E. Boudot-Lamotte, Paris 27; R. Braunmüller, Munich 15; British Museum, London 34, 50, 61, 88, 96; J. E. Bulloz, Paris 125; Rudolph Burckhardt, New York 151; Camera Press, London 98, front jacket centre left; Chicago Architectural Photo Co. 136; Courtauld Institute Galleries, London 131; Percival David Foundation of Chinese Art, London 37, 99; Dulwich College Picture Gallery 116; Egyptian Museum, West Berlin 12; Photographie Giraudon, Paris 28, 44, 46, 53, 58, 64, 85, 128; Hamlyn Group Picture Library 14, 17, 18, 19, 42, 45, 59, 76, 77, 82, 94, 95, 105, 111, 115, 123, 124, 126, 133, 138, 143, front jacket centre right, back jacket centre right; Hedrich-Blessing, Chicago 146; Fritz Henle–Photo Researchers Inc. 16; Lucien Hervé, Paris 142; Hans Hinz, Basle 1; Kunsthalle, Hamburg front jacket right, 139; Hirmer Verlag, Munich 8, 13, 23; Institut Géographique National, Paris 31; Sidney Janis Gallery, New York 152; A. F. Kersting, London 20, 24, 51, 63, 109, 118; Kodansha Ltd, Tokyo 33, 36, 65, 80, 83, 86, 87, 89, 91, 106, 113, 121, jacket front flap, back jacket centre left, back jacket right; Martin Koretz, London 153; Kunsthalle, Bremen endpapers; Kunsthistorisches Museum, Vienna 110; Mansell–Alinari illustration on page 5, 22; Bildarchiv Foto Marburg 84, 102; Marlborough Fine Art Ltd, London 150; Mas, Barcelona 3, 47, 93; Metropolitan Museum of Art, New York 52, 97; Arnoldo Mondadori Editore, Milan 148, front jacket left; Musée Rodin, Paris 134; Museum of Fine Arts, Boston 11: Museum of Fine Arts, Copenhagen 137; Museum of Modern Art, New York 140, 144; Museum für Völkerkunde, Munich 4, 7; Nationalgalerie, West Berlin 127; National Gallery, London 120; National Gallery of Art, Washington 92; National Museum, Tokyo 103; Palace Museum, Taiwan 38; Pergamon Museum, Berlin 21; Philadelphia Museum of Art 145; Josephine Powell, Rome 10, 41, 49; Réunion des Musées Nationaux, Paris 108, 119, 130; Marc Ribaud-Magnum, photo from the John Hillelson Agency 100; Rijksmuseum, Amsterdam 32; Professor Alfred Roth, Basle 141; M. Sakamoto, Tokyo 101; Scala, Florence 2, 39, 40, 43, 55, 56, 60, 66, 67, 72, 73, 78, 81, 90, 107, 112, 114, 122, 132, back jacket flap; The Rev. Professor R. V. Shoder, S. J., Chicago 26; Smithsonian Institution, Freer Gallery, Washington 48, illustration on pages 2–3; State Hermitage Museum, Leningrad 6; Ezra Stoller Associates, New York 155, back jacket left; Wim Swaan, New York 29; Tate Gallery, London 147, 154; Trinity College, Dublin illustration on page 4; Ulster Museum, Belfast 149; Yan, Toulouse 54.

Index